CRAVEN ARMS TO LLANDEILO

John Organ

Front Cover: A classic scene of the Central Wales Line is depicted at Builth Road High Level Station. Fowler 2-6-4T no. 42388 was recorded whilst hauling the 2.40pm Shrewsbury to Swansea service on 15th September 1949. (T.J.Edgington)

Rear Cover. An Arriva Trains Wales class 153 single car was viewed arriving at Craven Arms, with a Swansea to Shrewsbury service on 23rd April 2008. (M.J.Stretton)

Published September 2008

ISBN 978 1 906008 35 2

© Middleton Press, 2008

Design Deborah Esher

Published by
    Middleton Press
    Easebourne Lane
    Midhurst
    West Sussex
    GU29 9AZ
Tel: 01730 813169
Fax: 01730 812601
Email: info@middletonpress.co.uk
www.middletonpress.co.uk

Printed & bound by Biddles Ltd, Kings Lynn

INDEX

12	Broome	116	Glanrhyd Halt	114	Llangadog
19	Bucknell	16	Hopton Heath	80	Llangammarch
61	Builth Road	24	Knighton	36	Llangynllo
77	Cilmeri	32	Knucklas	111	Llanwrda
1	Craven Arms	38	Llanbister Road	81	Llanwrtyd
95	Cynghordy	117	Llandeilo	46	Pen-y-bont
42	Dolau	100	Llandovery	88	Sugar Loaf
78	Garth (Powys)	50	Llandrindod		

I. This diagram of the Central Wales Line shows the ownership of the various sections prior to 1923. (D.J.Smith/Town & Country Press)

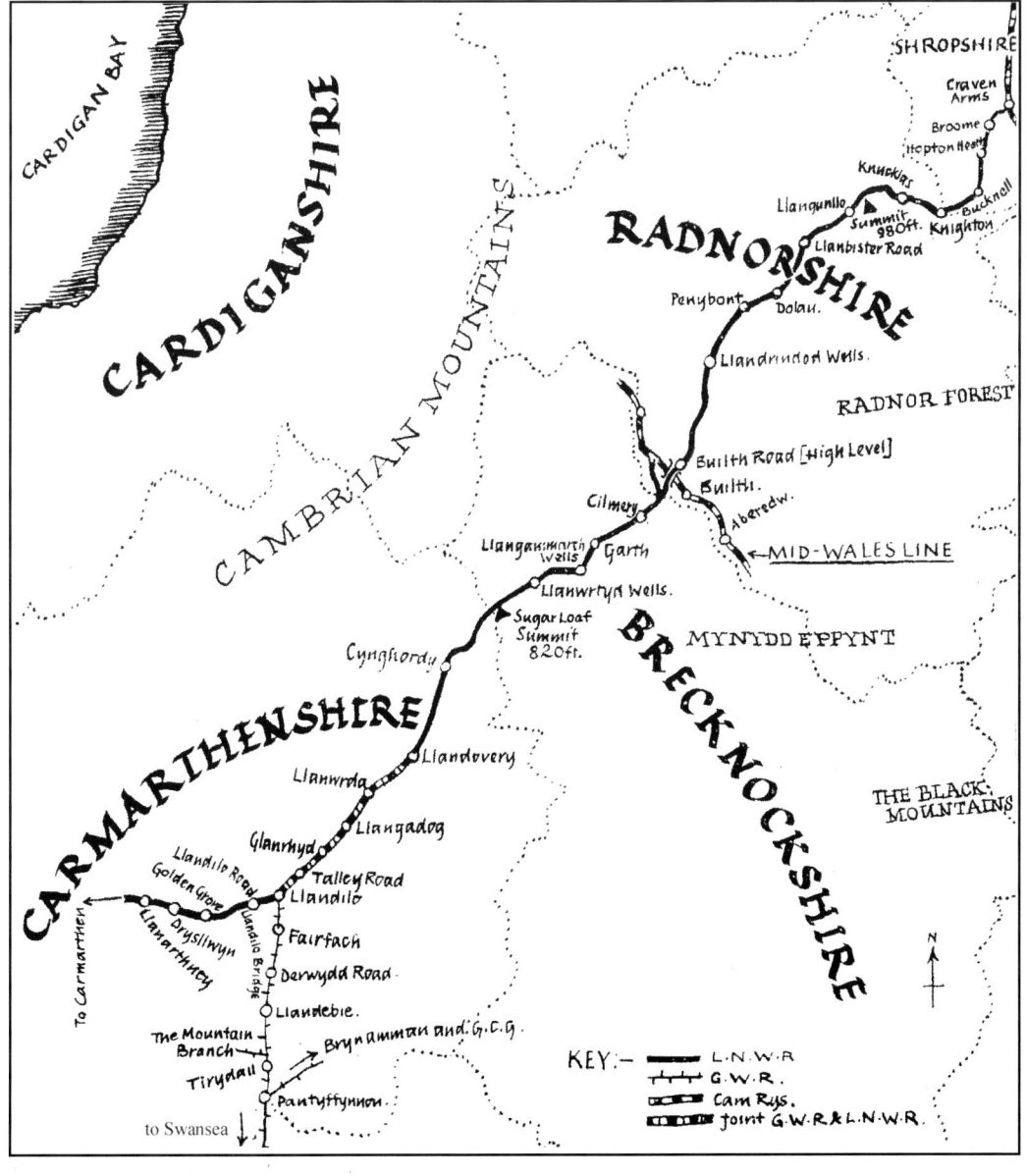

ACKNOWLEDGEMENTS

I am very grateful for the assistance received from the many photographers and collectors mentioned in the credits. In addition I must also thank R.K.Blenkowe, G.Croughton, J.Fozard, N.Langridge, N.Nicholson (WRRC) and T.Walsh (LOSA), who have also contributed in various ways. Finally, I must add a special word of thanks to my wife Brenda, who has once again tolerated my deep involvement with the project during the period of research and compilation.

GEOGRAPHICAL SETTING

From the once important and busy junction at Craven Arms, where our route connects with the "North and West" line linking Hereford and Shrewsbury, the Central Wales Line diverges at a junction a short distance to the south of the station. Passing through the rural landscape of Shropshire the line initially follows the valley of the River Onny, before proceeding in a southwesterly direction towards the River Teme near Bucknell. The first principal station is at the border town of Knighton, 12 miles from Craven Arms. Although the town is located in Powys, formerly Radnorshire, the station is situated in Shropshire, the border between England and Wales being passed immediately after leaving the down platform, where the line formerly changed from double to single track formation.

The line begins to climb through a thickly wooded area, whilst crossing the head of the Heyop Valley at the thirteen arch Knucklas Viaduct. The climb continues through the 645 yard long Llangunllo Tunnel, emerging at the highest point on the route at the 980ft Llangunllo Summit. After a long descent through Llanbister Road, where the former double track recommenced, the route proceeded via Dolau and Penybont Junction. Here the line became single again before passing through the 440 yard Penybont Tunnel after which the double track formation was regained as the route ran close to the River Ithon towards the major station at Llandrindod Wells, 31 miles from Craven Arms.

After leaving Llandrindod Wells, the line became single again as it passed through the quiet farming country of Mid Wales before arriving at Builth Road High Level Station, 38 miles from Craven Arms. Here the Central Wales Line crossed over the Cambrian (later GWR) Mid-Wales Line. South of the station was a connecting line completed by the LNWR that linked the two routes, whilst a motive power depot was located alongside the latter line.

Half a mile beyond Builth Road, our route crosses the River Wye over a two span wrought iron bridge. This was also the boundary between Radnorshire and Breconshire, although both are now part of Powys. The line climbs from the Wye Valley via two short tunnels before descending to the valley of the River Irfon at Llangammarch Wells. After another short climb on a gradient of 1 in 80, the line runs on the level in a westerly direction to Llanwrtyd Wells, 45 miles from the commencement of the journey.

After crossing the River Irfon, a long ascent on another 1 in 80 gradient takes the line to Sugar Loaf Summit, 820 ft above sea level. There then begins a descent on a gradient of 1 in 70 through the single bore 1000 yard long Sugar Loaf Tunnel, the county boundary between Breconshire (Powys) and Carmarthenshire (now part of Dyfed) being passed at the mid-point of the tunnel. There then follows a four-mile long descent via a series of sweeping curves on a gradient of 1 in 60 before crossing the 283 yard long Cynghordy Viaduct. The landscape is now primarily heath land, mainly populated by sheep grazing among the stunted gorse bushes. After the small station at Cynghordy, the route adopts a southwesterly course as it follows the River Bran to the busy agricultural and market town of Llandovery, 59 miles from Craven Arms.

Departing from Llandovery, the single track proceeds in a southwesterly direction on a falling gradient amid the low wooded hills of the Vale of Towy. Ultimately the River Towy is crossed on a four-arch girder bridge, following a stretch of track laid on marsh and bog, before Llangadog is reached six miles after leaving Llandovery. The River Towy is again crossed together with two tributaries of the same river to the north of Glanrhyd, before the largest intermediate station on the Central Wales Line at Llandeilo is approached after a further five miles. Llandeilo (originally named Llandilo), 70 miles from Craven Arms, was also the location of a junction from which a LNWR branch, 13 miles in length, diverged from the Central Wales route in a westerly direction towards Carmarthen.

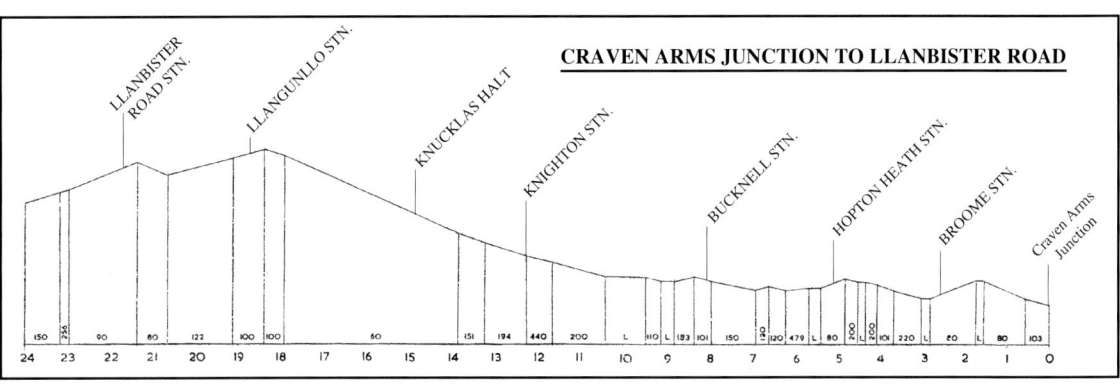

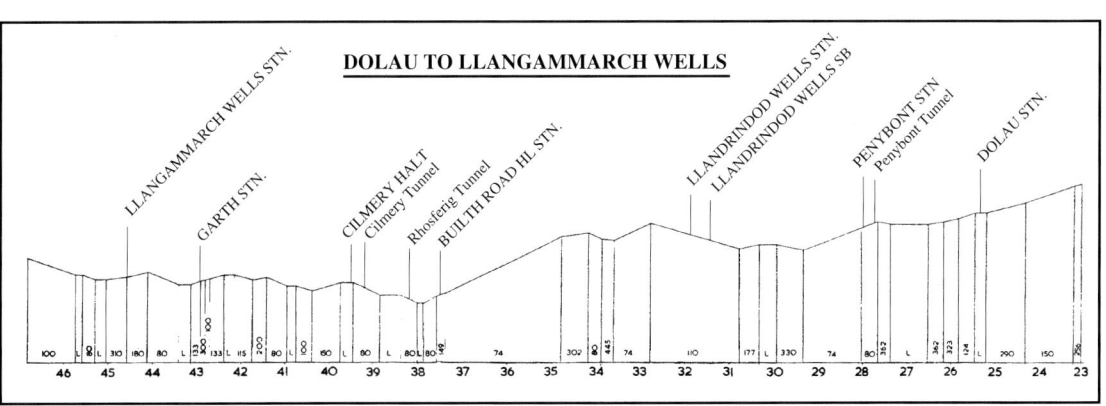

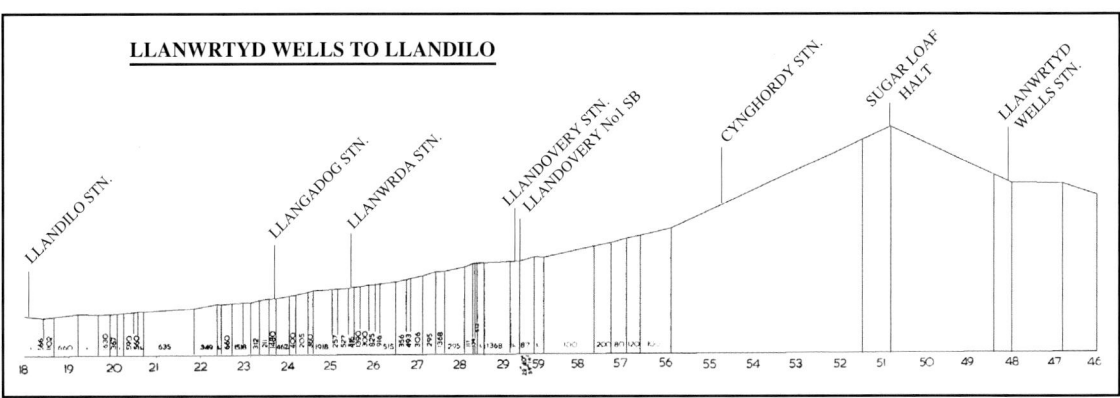

Gradient profiles - Note - Mileage is recorded from Craven Arms to Llandovery (LNWR section) and from Llandilo Junction, near Llanelli, to Llandovery (GWR section).

HISTORICAL BACKGROUND

The route between Craven Arms and Llandeilo had its origins in four separate undertakings, three of which were amalgamated within a decade of the opening of the first section. Craven Arms & Stokesay station had opened on 21st April 1852 as part of the Shrewsbury & Hereford Railway. On 6th March 1861, the Knighton Railway was opened throughout from a junction created at the south end of the station, known as Central Wales Junction. The 12 miles long line to the Radnorshire town of Knighton was built at the instigation of a consortium of local landowners and businessmen. The route between Central Wales Junction at Craven Arms and Knighton was doubled in 1871.

On 13th August 1859, an independent company known as the Central Wales Railway was incorporated by an Act of Parliament, many of the directors being those involved with the Knighton Railway. The 19 miles route from Knighton to the flourishing spa town of Llandrindod Wells finally opened on 10th October 1865.

During the course of the construction of the CWR, a further Act of Parliament in 1860 authorised the construction of a line linking Llandrindod Wells and the important market town and livestock centre at Llandovery. Known as the Central Wales Extension Railway, the 28 miles long route was opened on 8th October 1868.

During the period that the final section of line to Llandovery was under construction, the three companies amalgamated and were leased to the London & North Western Railway (LNWR), which already had running rights over the completed sections of the route. On 25th June 1868, the three companies were finally incorporated as part of the LNWR. The London Midland & Scottish Railway (LMS) owned the line from 1923 until nationalisation in 1948. The route then became part of British Railways Western Region, although former LMS motive power continued to be used until the demise of steam during the 1960s.

The line between Llandovery and Llandeilo predated the lines to the north, having been authorised by an Act of Parliament on 10th July 1854 and known as the Vale of Towy Railway. The 11 miles route was opened to traffic on 1st April 1858, but was leased from the outset to the Llanelly Railroad (later renamed Railway) and Dock Company which had completed its line to Llandilo in 1857. The Llanelly Railway was absorbed by the Great Western Railway in 1889, the GWR understandably staking a claim for the Vale of Towy Railway in which the LNWR also had a vested interest. The result was that the Llandovery to Llandilo section was henceforth controlled by the LNWR (LMS) and GWR as a joint operation, which continued until 1948.

In 1964, the route was reduced to that of a "basic railway" with the removal of the double track sections. The minor intermediate stations were either downgraded to unstaffed halts or closed completely. All freight services were withdrawn after August 1964. The basic DMU operated passenger service is now marketed as "The Heart of Wales Line" and is currently operated by Arriva Trains Wales, who took over the franchise from Regional Railways in December 2003.

The section between Llandovery and Llandeilo was closed to all traffic between 19th October 1987 and 31st October 1988. This was as a result of the bridge over the River Towy to the north of Glanrhyd being washed away by severe floods. Unfortunately the bridge collapsed just as a DMU was about to cross the structure, with fatal consequences. This was the only serious accident that has occurred on the Central Wales Line during its history.

All stationes opened with, or within a year of, the line unless otherwise indicated. Note: The original spellings for Llandilo and Llanelly have been used in their historical context with reference to period between 1857 and 1948 described above.

PASSENGER SERVICES

When the Knighton Railway began operations in 1861, three trains in each direction were operated daily between Craven Arms and Knighton on weekdays only. By the time the route of the line south to Llandovery was opened in 1868, an end-on connection was made with the existing lines from Swansea and Llanelli. Consequently, the majority of passenger trains running over the line to the north of Llandeilo were through trains between Shrewsbury and Swansea.

In 1922, during the last year of LNWR operation, five trains were listed on through services to Swansea. In addition two trains operated from Shrewsbury to Builth Road and one to Llandovery. During the 1930s, a through carriage was attached to the 9.30am departure from Swansea, which was detached at Shrewsbury and coupled to a train for Stafford. Here it was added to the up " Mid-Day Scot", arriving at Euston during the late afternoon. Bearing in mind that a direct GWR service between Swansea and Paddington offered a far quicker journey to London, this somewhat indirect service appeared to be of little value! The down "Manxman" that departed from Euston at 10.40am also detached a carriage at Stafford for a service in the reverse direction.

A similar five train service was operated throughout the LMS and BR era, until the closure of Swansea Victoria station in 1964. Services declined during the early 1960s to the extent that by 1964 the only long distance through train was the "York Mail".

Since 1964, the passenger service has been operated by DMUs between Shrewsbury and Llanelli, where reversal is necessary for the remainder of the journey to Swansea. For many years the five weekday train tradition was revived, this now being reduced to four trains. Sunday services are restricted to two trains in each direction.

1923 Bradshaw showing Southbound services.

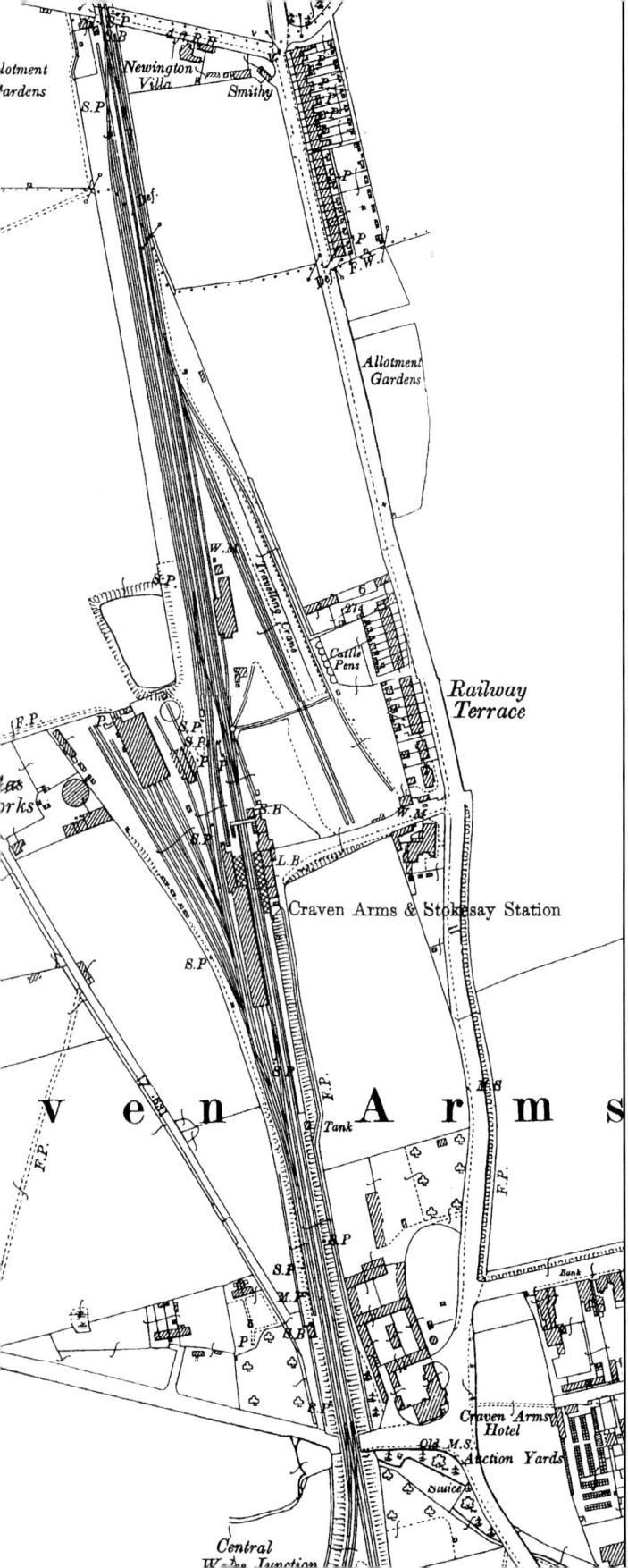

CRAVEN ARMS

II. The 1903 survey at 15ins to 1 mile shows the extensive complex situated on the joint LNWR and GWR Shrewsbury to Hereford line. The main trunk road linking the two towns (A49 since 1919) can be seen on the right passing through the village of Newington, which ultimately became part of Craven Arms. The name was derived from that of an inn situated between Newington and Newtown, a village a short distance to the south. The goods loop running behind the up platform is clearly shown, as is the LNWR locomotive depot and associated sidings. More important for this publication is the location of Central Wales Junction to the south of the station, near to the Craven Arms Hotel.

↗ 1. The station was also a junction for trains from the Bishops Castle Railway until its demise in 1934. This is its 0-6-0 *Carlisle*, which is about to depart at 11.20am on 30th May 1932. (H.C.Casserley)

→ 2. Fowler 2-6-4T no. 42305 is viewed arriving at the station whilst hauling the 7.45am Swansea to Shrewsbury service on 10th September 1949. Note that the locomotive had received its BR number but still retained its LMS insignia. These popular locomotives were commonly used on the Central Wales route for many years, until they were replaced by later BR variants during the 1960s. (H.C.Casserley)

→ 3. This is a view of Craven Arms & Stokesay station, as it was originally named, looking north from the down platform. This view was recorded during the 1950s, when the station complex was far more extensive than the current layout. (Lens of Sutton coll.)

4. The down platform was recorded on the same occasion. The extensive name boards providing information of the various connections provided from the station are clearly shown. (Lens of Sutton coll.)

5. Stanier 2-8-0 no. 48309 was photographed as it hauled a heavy northbound freight train along the station avoiding line, which formerly ran behind the up platform. This view dates from 1959. (D.K.Jones coll.)

6. Behind the photographer in the previous view was the large stone-built locomotive shed. Originally provided with four roads with a total capacity of five engines, by the time that this view was obtained during the late 1950s, it had been reduced to three roads. (Lens of Sutton coll.)

7. The majority of trains from Swansea continued their journey north, terminating at Shrewsbury. 2-6-4T no. 42385 was recorded in the up platform whilst hauling the 6.15am service from Swansea to Shrewsbury on 30th April 1960. (R.Patterson)

8. Class 5MT 4-6-0 no.73035 was viewed as it arrived at the up platform whilst hauling a train from Swansea on a very wet day in August 1961. (D.K.Jones coll.)

9. The rationalisation that transformed the appearance of Craven Arms station after 1964 is evident as a two car DMU waits in the up platform whilst working the 12.25pm Swansea to Shrewsbury service on 12th July 1976. (T.Heavyside)

10. The current single line of the Central Wales route is visible to the right, immediately to the south of the up platform. Central Wales Junction was formerly a double track layout approximately adjacent to the last carriage of the train. No.37431 was hauling the 2.00pm service from Cardiff to Manchester on the North and West route when this view was obtained on 1st October 1988. (T.Heavyside)

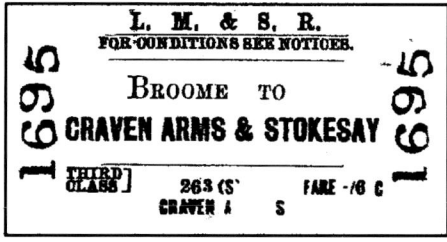

11.   Our final view of this important station shows a three car DMU set departing from the up platform as the 3.25pm Swansea to Shrewsbury service at 7.00pm on 8th May 1989. (P.G.Barnes)

Additional views of Craven Arms can be found in the *Shrewsbury to Ludlow* album and also *Craven Arms to Wellington*.

BROOME

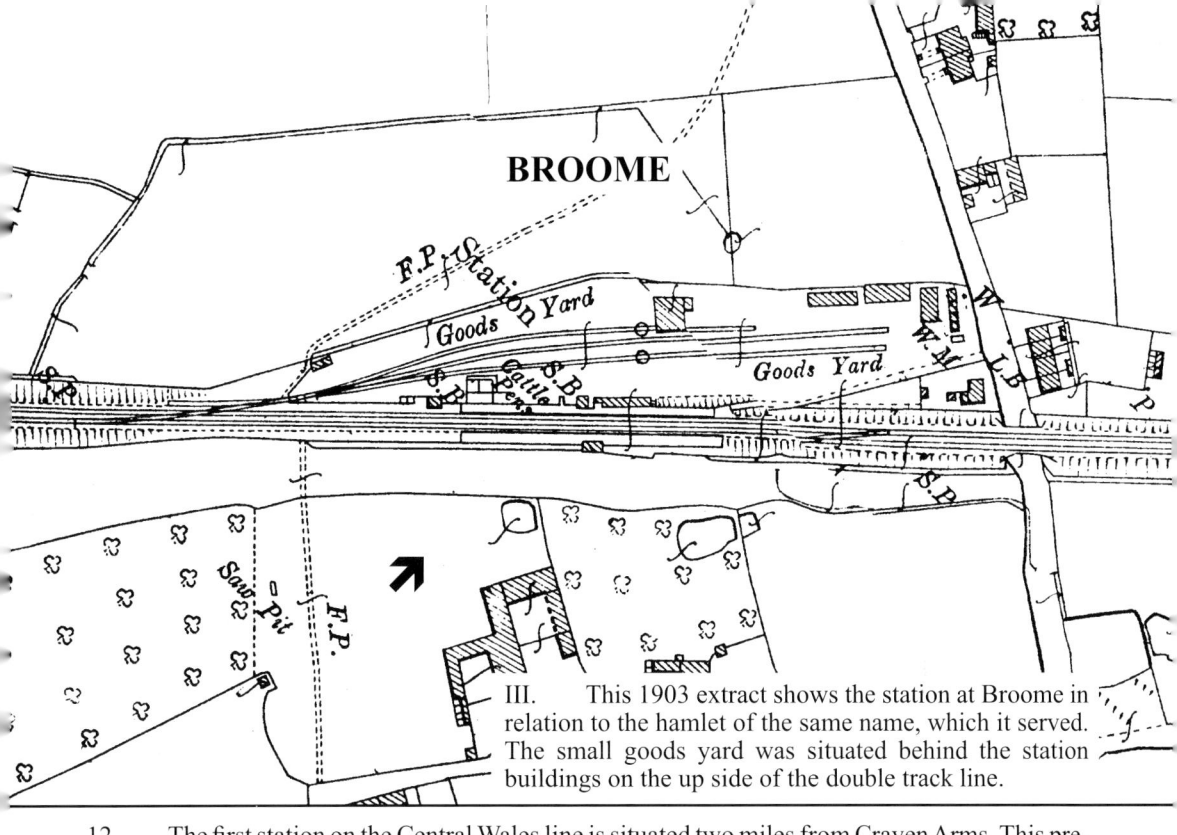

III. This 1903 extract shows the station at Broome in relation to the hamlet of the same name, which it served. The small goods yard was situated behind the station buildings on the up side of the double track line.

12. The first station on the Central Wales line is situated two miles from Craven Arms. This pre-grouping view of the wayside station features the original signal box situated on the up platform. This was later replaced by a larger structure to the south of the station, as shown in photograph 14. (Lens of Sutton coll.)

13. Fowler 2-6-4T no.42394 was recorded as it drew to a halt at the up platform whilst hauling the 6.15am service from Swansea to Shrewsbury on 15th September 1949. (T.J.Edgington)

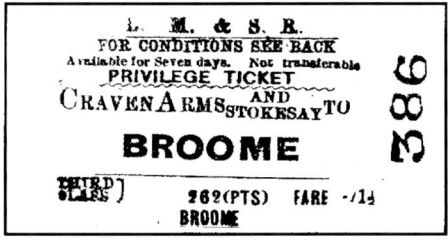

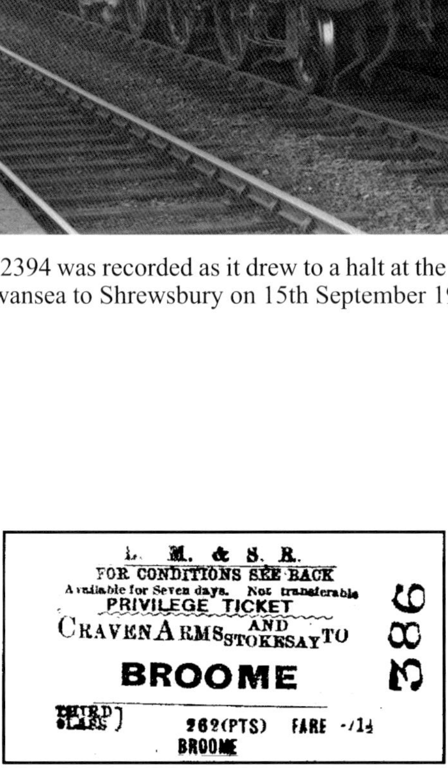

14. The down platform was of wooden construction, whilst the station building on the up side was of wooden clad construction, as clearly shown in this view of the station looking south on 27th April 1963. (R.Patterson)

15. Whilst traversing the single line of the latter day Central Wales route, a two car DMU was viewed passing the halt that now occupies the former station site at Broome. The train formed the 10.43am Shrewsbury to Swansea service on 10th May 1989. (P.G.Barnes)

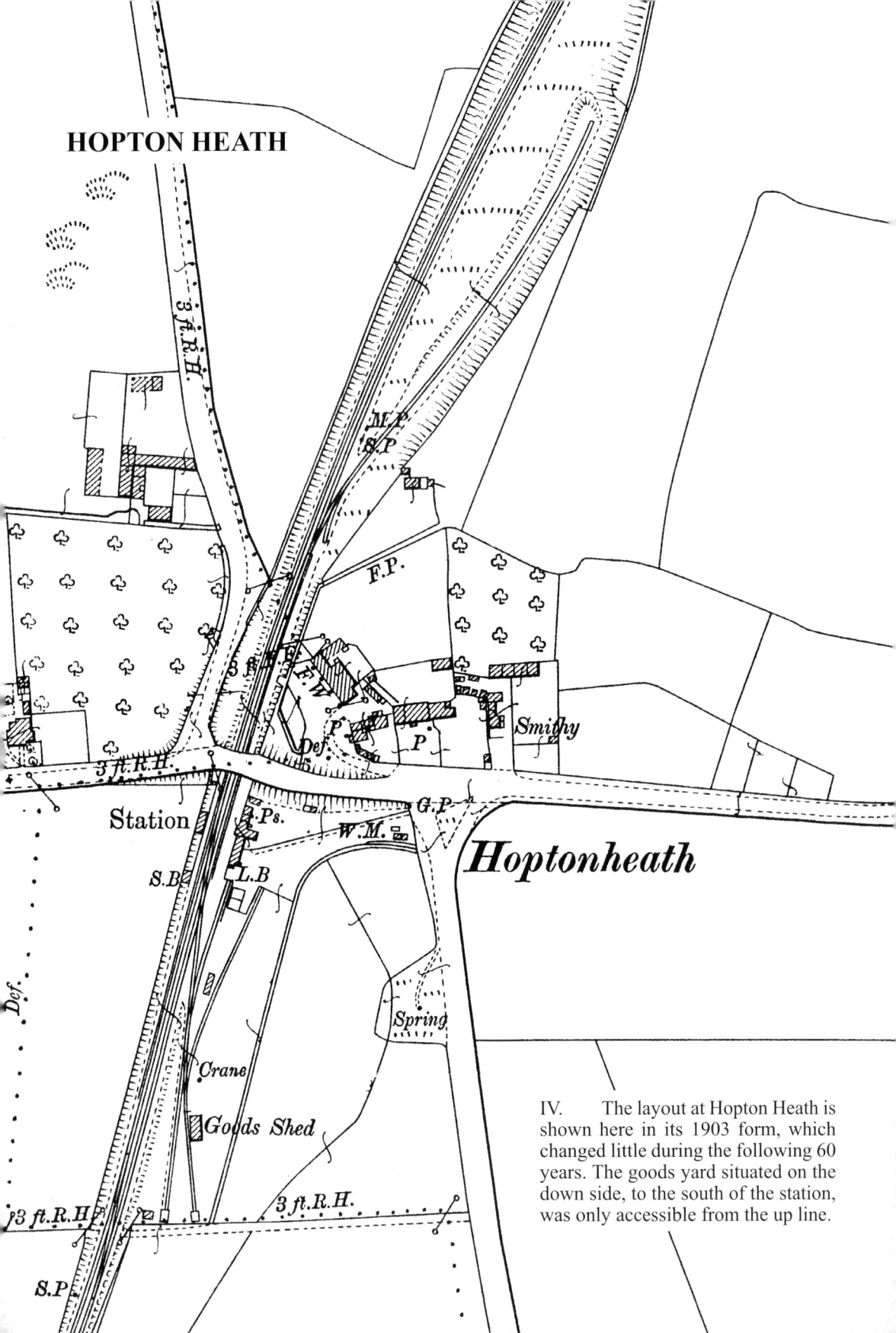

IV. The layout at Hopton Heath is shown here in its 1903 form, which changed little during the following 60 years. The goods yard situated on the down side, to the south of the station, was only accessible from the up line.

16.   This station was located three miles from Broome and featured a solid brick building with a small goods yard on the down side. This view looking north towards Craven Arms was recorded on 27th April 1963, by which time the goods yard was definitely no longer in use. (R.Patterson)

17.   Viewed from the road bridge seen in the previous photograph, 2-6-4T no. 80097 was recorded as it arrived at the up platform whilst hauling the 6.15am Swansea to Shrewsbury service on the same occasion. The truncated sidings leading to the goods yard, are visible on the down side. (R.Patterson)

18. The down platform was recorded after the line had been singled in 1965. This view of the station, which is now a private residence, was photographed in 1969.
(M.Morton Lloyd/WRRC coll.)

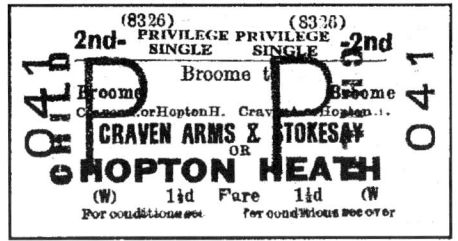

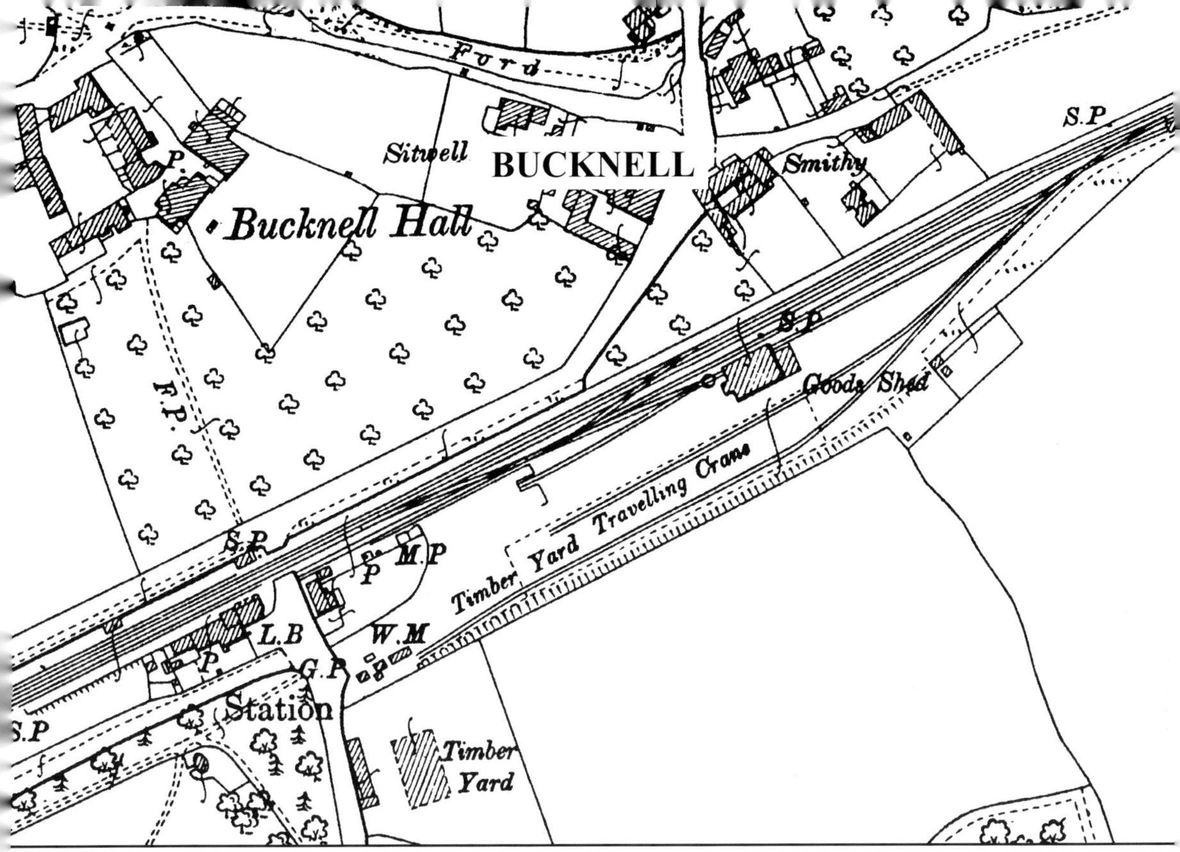

V.   The extensive station complex is seen in 1903. The delightful village was served by an equally delightful station, the main building of which has fortunately survived – albeit as a private residence. The passenger and freight sections of the complex were separated by the level crossing, although an additional small goods yard was later installed behind the station building.

19.   Situated eight miles from Craven Arms, this attractive station served the adjoining village located in a beautiful setting. The up platform was recorded during the early years of the 20th century when a LNWR "Jumbo" class 2-4-0 was photographed arriving at the station with a Shrewsbury bound excursion between 1905 and 1910. (Lens of Sutton coll.)

20. The fine London & North Western signal box near the level crossing is prominent in this scene. Class 5MT 4-6-0 no.73003 was viewed as it departed from the station with the 7.25am service from Swansea on 27th April 1963. (R.Patterson)

21. This view from the same occasion as the previous photograph, looking towards Craven Arms, shows the stone built neo-gothic styled station building on the down side. The small goods yard was located behind the building whilst the up platform was provided with a wooden waiting shelter. (R.Patterson)

22. Following the station being reduced to an unstaffed halt in 1964, the signal box remained open for use as a ground frame and operation of the level crossing gates. The following year the goods facilities were withdrawn and the goods yard behind the station building removed. Concurrently the line was singled, reducing the box to level crossing operation only, until 1978 when it was demolished and the gates replaced with lights. This view was obtained on 21st June 1969. (E.Wilmshurst)

23. Steam hauled charter trains have become a common occurrence during the last decade. Class 5MT 4-6-0 no. 45407 and 4MT 2-6-0 no. 76079 were recorded as they passed through the station whilst hauling the Crewe to Newport leg of a tour that originated from Leicester on 19th April 2008. (J.F.Organ)

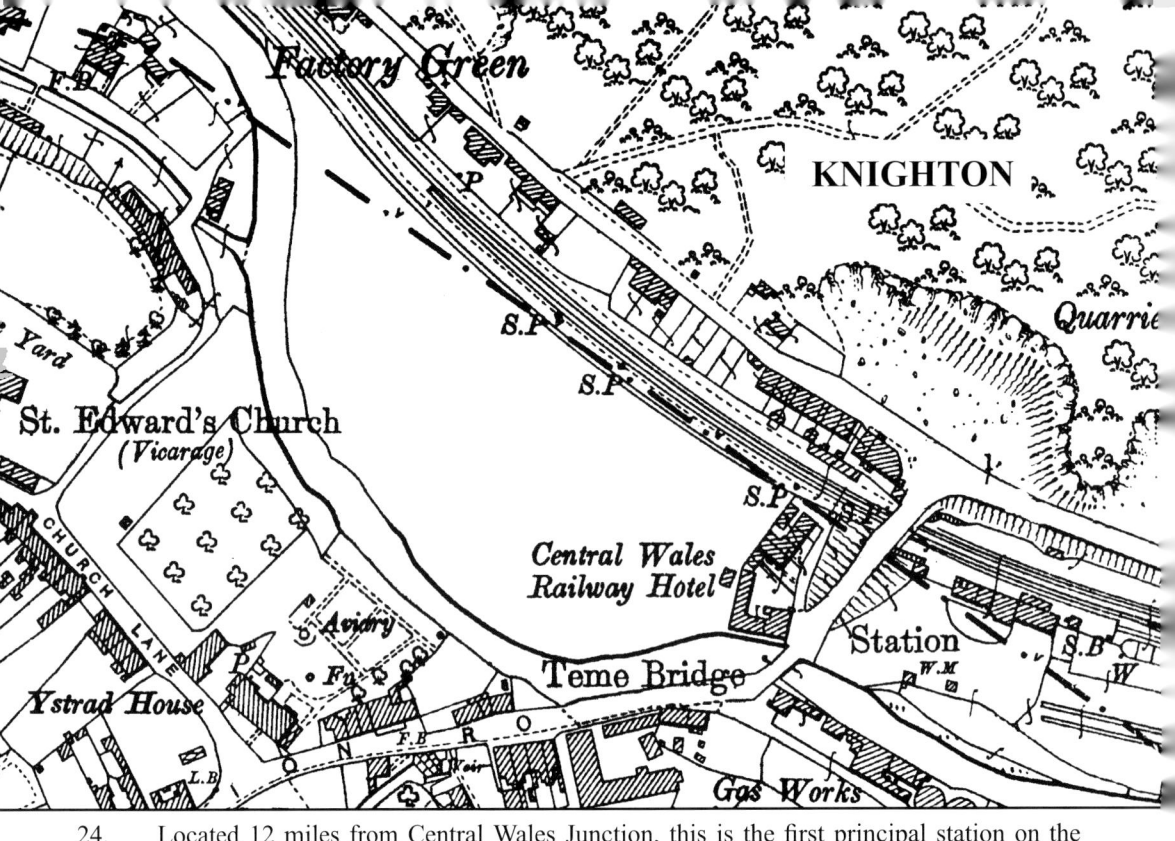

24. Located 12 miles from Central Wales Junction, this is the first principal station on the route. Situated on the county boundary, the station was located in Shropshire although it served the Radnorshire town of Knighton. This splendid view from 1909/10 shows a LNWR Bowen-Cooke 4-6-2T, no. 2667, in the up platform awaiting the signal to proceed towards Craven Arms. (G.M.Perkins/R.Carpenter coll.)

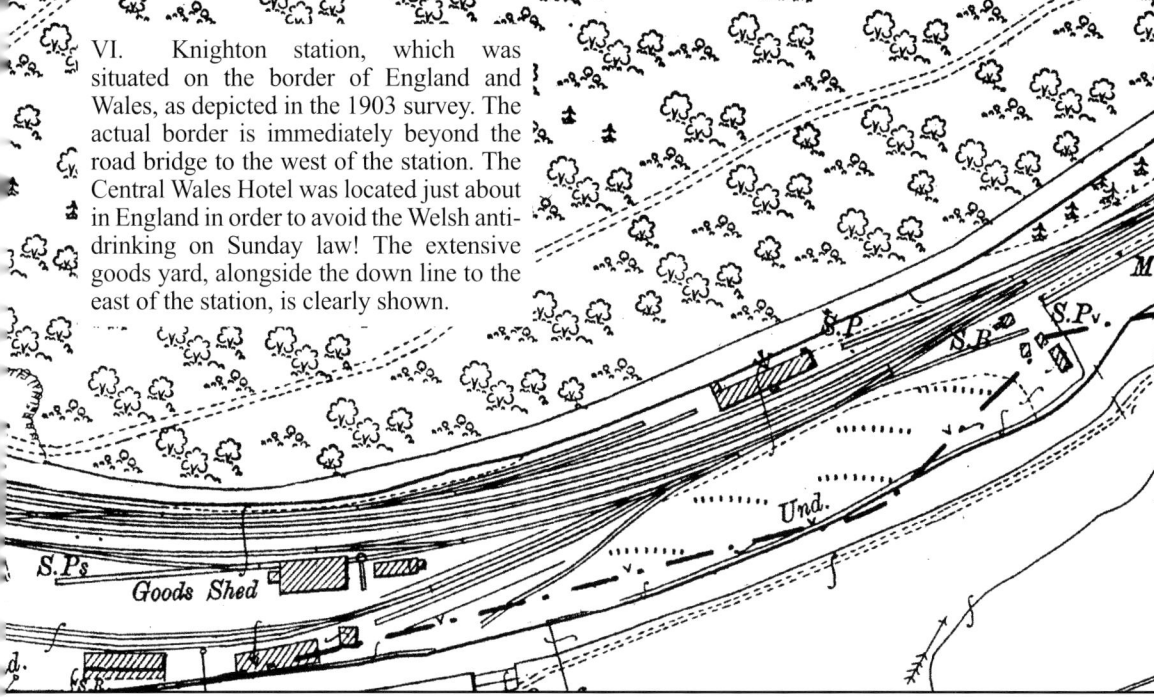

VI. Knighton station, which was situated on the border of England and Wales, as depicted in the 1903 survey. The actual border is immediately beyond the road bridge to the west of the station. The Central Wales Hotel was located just about in England in order to avoid the Welsh anti-drinking on Sunday law! The extensive goods yard, alongside the down line to the east of the station, is clearly shown.

25. Viewed from the bridge to the southwest of the complex, former LNWR 0-8-0 no. 9358 was recorded approaching the station with a Craven Arms to Llandovery freight train on 15th September 1949. The goods yard and shed can be seen in the distance alongside the down lines. (T.J.Edgington)

26.   The same train is pictured as it drew to a halt in the down platform, before it resumed its journey south into Radnorshire. The footbridge from which this view was obtained was attached to the parapet of the roadbridge. (T.J.Edgington)

27.   Fowler 2-6-4T no. 42385 was photographed as it arrived in the up platform whilst hauling the 7.45am Swansea to Shrewsbury service on 15th September 1949. The footbridge referred to in the previous photograph can be seen above the second carriage. (T.J.Edgington)

28. Compared to the facilities on the down side of the station, the up platform was adorned with a very modest waiting shelter. This view of the up side was recorded from a Swansea bound train on 11th September 1952. (H.C.Casserley)

29. The impressive stone built Victorian building was located on the down platform with the goods yard situated to the northeast of the station alongside the southbound line. A single road engine shed was located on the opposite side of the running lines. The station complex was seen to good advantage in this view from 27th April 1963. The station building has survived, but is now in use for commercial purposes. (R.Patterson)

30. In 1965 the line was singled, which rendered the up platform obsolete. As a result the 31mile section between Craven Arms and Llandrindod Wells became the longest stretch of single-track railway in Great Britain. A passing loop was reinstated at the station in 1990 in order to allow more flexibility. The 10.05 Swansea to Shrewsbury DMU was viewed in the former down platform of the much reduced station on 13th June 1983. (T.Heavyside)

31. The same unit seen in the previous photograph was recorded as it approached the station from the west with its Shrewsbury bound service. Note the headlamp attached to the front of the DMU, a requirement for all motive power working on the Central Wales Line since 1965. (T.Heavyside)

KNUCKLAS

32.   Knucklas is situated two miles beyond Knighton, at the head of the Heyop Valley. The now demolished buildings were recorded on 28th April 1963, with the impressive Knucklas Viaduct in the distance to the west. (R.Patterson)

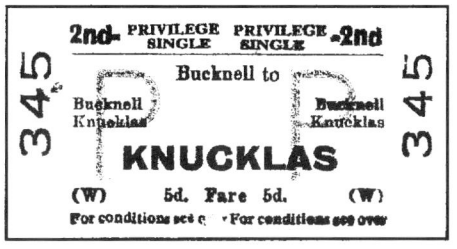

33. A more detailed view of Knucklas Viaduct is seen from the down side of the structure. One of the four castellated towers that "protect" the approaches can be seen beyond the last arch in this scene recorded on 13th June 1983. (T.Heavyside)

34. Class 5MT 4-6-0 no. 44767 was recorded as it hauled a rail tour across the viaduct, heading towards Llandovery and South Wales on 23rd May 1993. The 13 arch viaduct is still a notable landmark on the Central Wales Line and is famed for the circular towers at each end of the structure. (D.Trevor Rowe)

EAST OF LLANGUNLLO

35. A Swansea bound train hauled by class 3F 0-6-0 no. 43600 and class 4MT 2-6-4T no. 42307, approaches Llangunllo Tunnel and Summit on 11th September 1952. Three milk tank wagons can be seen between the locomotives and the leading carriage. (H.C.Casserley)

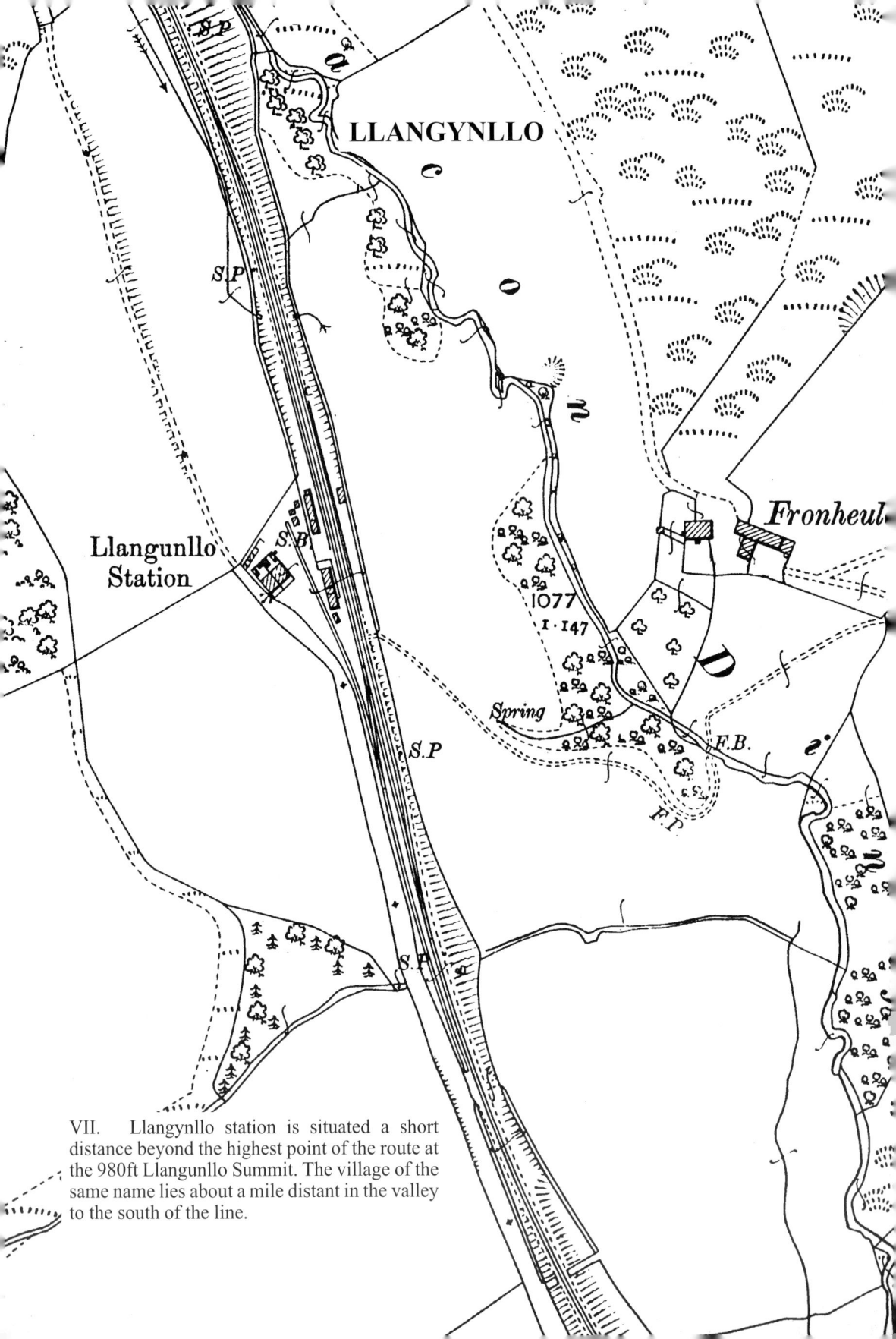

VII. Llangynllo station is situated a short distance beyond the highest point of the route at the 980ft Llangunllo Summit. The village of the same name lies about a mile distant in the valley to the south of the line.

36. The isolated station, 18 miles from Craven Arms, was recorded from the same train as seen in the previous photograph. This view shows the LNWR waiting rooms on the up platform and the station house, which also housed the signal box. In the distance 0-6-0 no.43600, which had assisted the train on the ascent from Knighton, can be seen on the up line after being detached from the train. (H.C.Casserley)

37. The 12.27pm Swansea to Shrewsbury DMU service was recorded as it approached the by then unmanned station at Llangynllo, whilst climbing the final stretch of 1 in100 to Llangunllo Summit on 13th June 1983. (T.Heavyside)

LLANBISTER ROAD

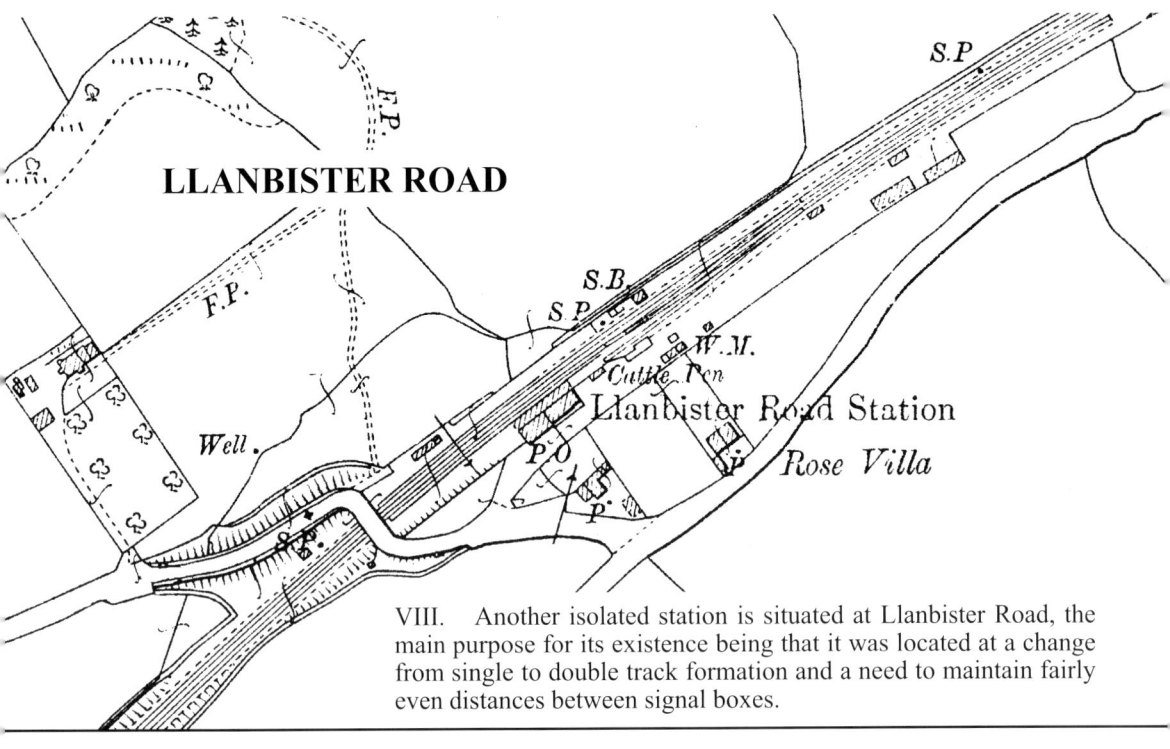

VIII. Another isolated station is situated at Llanbister Road, the main purpose for its existence being that it was located at a change from single to double track formation and a need to maintain fairly even distances between signal boxes.

38. Apart from the station loop at Llangunllo, the formation was single track from Knighton. Located 22 miles from Central Wales Junction, this station was situated on the long descent from Llangunllo Summit at the point where the double track formation re-commenced. In this elevated view of the station looking northeast towards Craven Arms, the start of the single-track section can be seen beyond the signal box. This scene was recorded on 27th April 1963, featuring another LNWR station building and the hills of the Radnor Forest in the distance. (R.Patterson)

39. Class 5MT no. 73026 was recorded as it departed from the station whilst hauling the 9.45am Swansea to Shrewsbury service on the same occasion. The start of the single line section was situated behind the photographer. (R.Patterson)

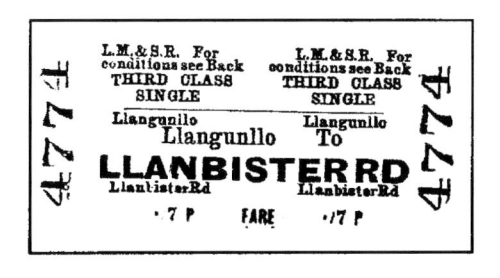

40. The station approach was showing signs of neglect when it was photographed on 20th September 1969. The main part of the building survives as a private residence. (M.Morton Lloyd/WRRC coll.)

41. When this scene was pictured on 14th February 1970, the line had been singled through the station and much of the infrastructure demolished. The former up platform continues to serve as an unstaffed station. (E.Wilmshurst)

DOLAU

42. A characteristic LMS station name board is clearly in evidence in this view of the up platform at this delightful spot. Situated 25 miles from Craven Arms, this scene was recorded on 11th September 1952. (H.C.Casserley)

43. A more detailed view of the layout dates from 27th April 1963. Prominent features are the wooden passenger shelters and the signal box adjacent to the level crossing, immediately to the north of the station. (R.Patterson)

44. A typically LNWR signal box protected the northern approach to the small station. The structure, with the Baptist Chapel immediately to the rear, was viewed after the line had been singled and the station reduced in status to an unmanned station on 21st June 1969. The box was demolished in 1978 when the crossing gates were replaced by lights. (E.Wilmshurst)

45. This view of the level crossing and signal box is from 20th September 1969, with the gates firmly closed against rail traffic. (M.Morton Lloyd/WRRC coll.)

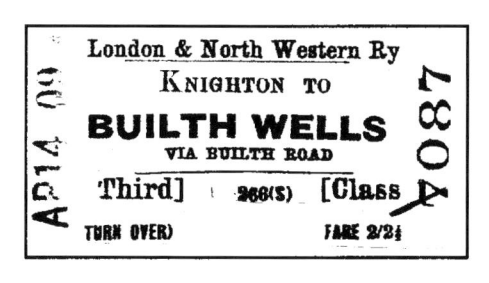

London & North Western Ry
KNIGHTON TO
BUILTH WELLS
VIA BUILTH ROAD
Third] 268(S) [Class
TURN OVER) FARE 2/2½

PEN-Y-BONT

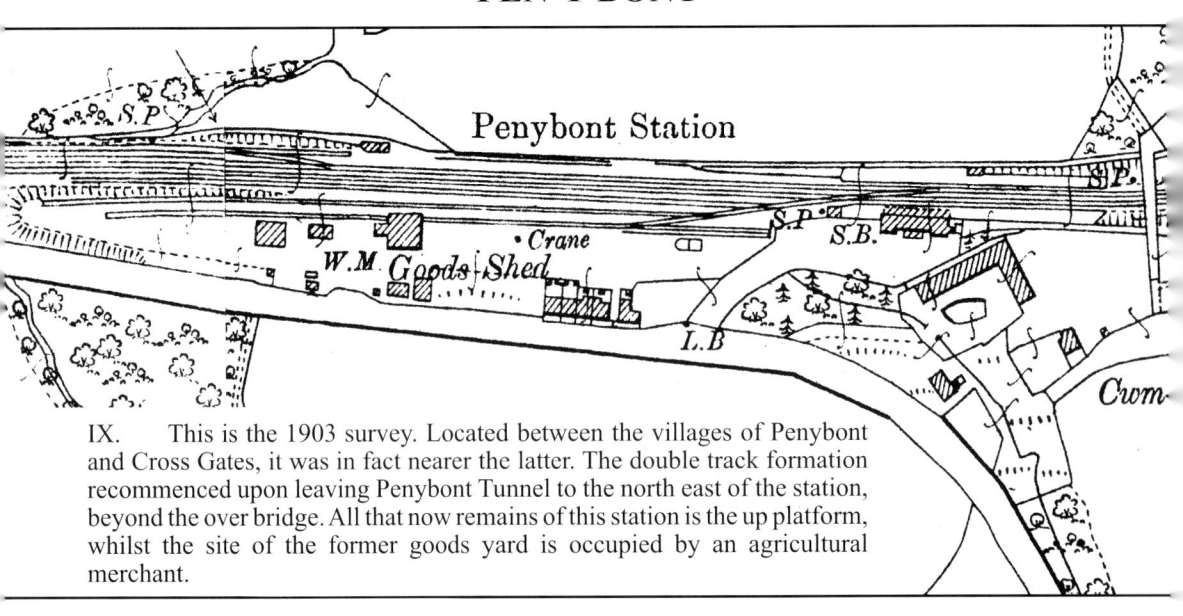

IX. This is the 1903 survey. Located between the villages of Penybont and Cross Gates, it was in fact nearer the latter. The double track formation recommenced upon leaving Penybont Tunnel to the north east of the station, beyond the over bridge. All that now remains of this station is the up platform, whilst the site of the former goods yard is occupied by an agricultural merchant.

46. South of Dolau, at a location named Penybont Junction, another section of single-track formation began for three miles, via Penybont Tunnel, to Penybont Station. In our first view of this station, class 5MT 4-6-0 no. 73095 was photographed as it left the single track whilst approaching the down platform at the head of the 6.00pm Shrewsbury to Swansea service on 15th June 1963. (R.Patterson)

47.	A view of the station, looking south, was taken on 27th April 1963. Prominent structures are the LNWR styled station buildings on the down platform, with the signal box beyond, and the small wooden shelter on the up platform. The double track formation can be seen heading towards Llandrindod Wells. (R.Patterson)

48.	Another class 5MT 4-6-0, no. 73035, is seen from the over bridge arriving at the up platform whilst hauling the 12.20pm Swansea to Shrewsbury service on the same occasion as the previous photograph. (R.Patterson)

49. A winter scene at Penybont was recorded as a southbound DMU passed through the remains of the station. Only the up platform survives on the now singled line, as shown in this view from 14th February 1970. (E.Wilmshurst)

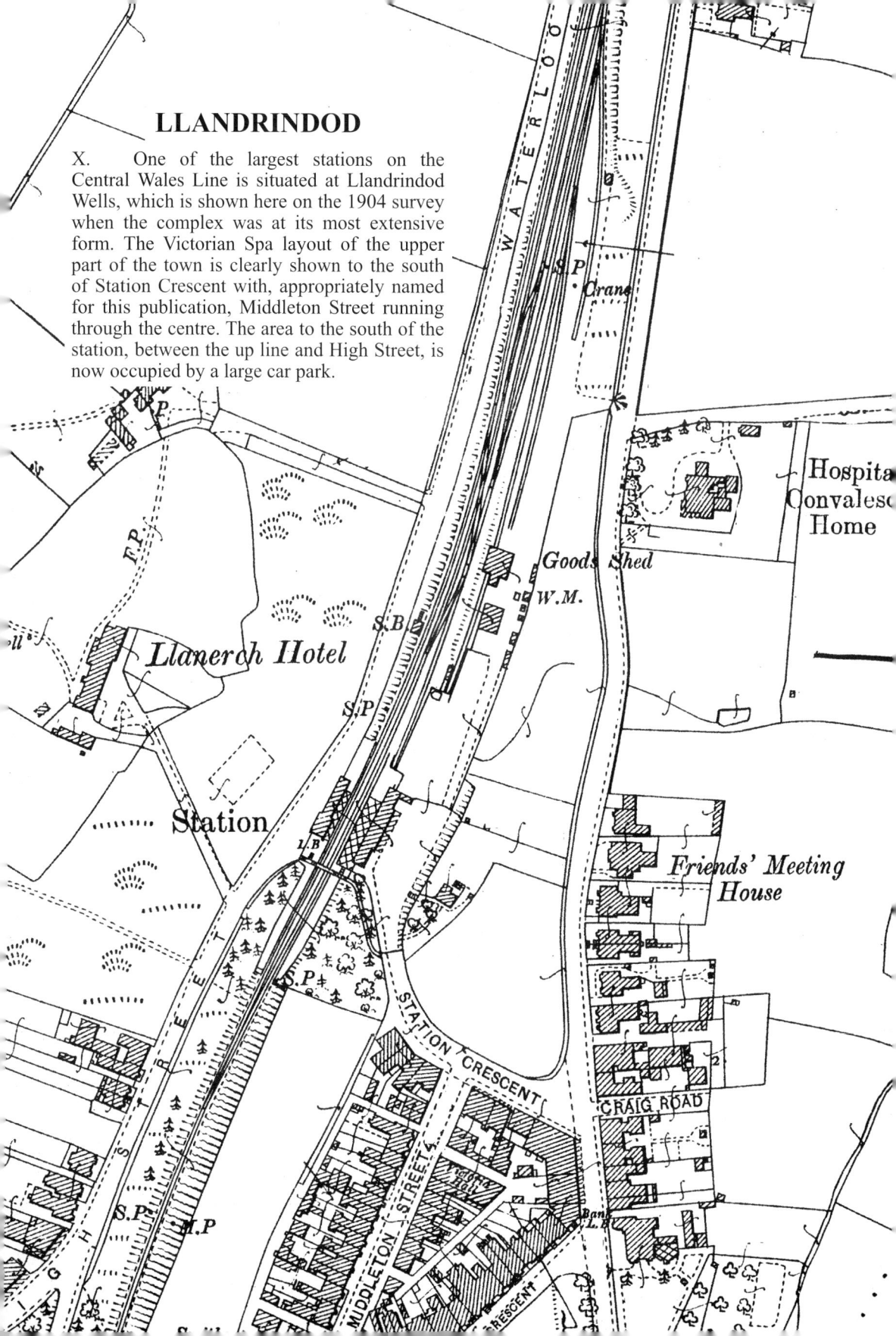

LLANDRINDOD

X. One of the largest stations on the Central Wales Line is situated at Llandrindod Wells, which is shown here on the 1904 survey when the complex was at its most extensive form. The Victorian Spa layout of the upper part of the town is clearly shown to the south of Station Crescent with, appropriately named for this publication, Middleton Street running through the centre. The area to the south of the station, between the up line and High Street, is now occupied by a large car park.

50.   Situated 31 miles from Central Wales Junction, the flourishing spa town was developed during the mid 19th century. As a consequence it boasted one of the major intermediate stations on the route. For three years it was the southern terminal of the original Central Wales Railway, before the extension to Llandovery was opened in 1868. An early 20th century view of the station shows a train hauled by a pair of LNWR 2-4-2Ts approaching the up platform in 1905, where a many passengers were awaiting its arrival. (M.Morton Lloyd/WRRC coll.)

51.   A view of the station looking north was obtained from the footbridge, as former LNWR 0-8-0 no. 9358 hauls a Llandovery bound freight train from the extensive goods yard on 15th September 1949. (T.J.Edgington)

52. Class 4MT 2-6-4T no. 42394 pauses with its train at the down platform, whilst hauling the 2.20pm Craven Arms to Llandovery service on the same occasion as the previous photograph. (T.J.Edgington)

53. Despite the rationalised track layout, the station infrastructure was still complete when this view looking south was recorded on 2nd August 1963. (E.Wilmshurst)

54. The exterior of the station has changed little during the ensuing years, as depicted in this view of the down side entrance in Station Crescent on 2nd October 1982. (E.Wilmshurst)

55. By the early 1980s the platform awnings had been removed reducing the appearance of the station to that of a minor halt. A two car DMU arrives at the former down platform operating the 12.25pm Swansea to Shrewsbury service on 2nd October 1982. (E.Wilmshurst)

56. A southbound DMU is seen as it approached the station from the north with a Shrewsbury to Swansea service on 13th June 1983. The A4081 to Rhayader, passes over the level crossing adjacent to the signal box in the background. (T.Heavyside)

57. The passing loop was reinstated in 1986. However the replacement awnings, which were previously situated at the local council offices, were still unglazed at the time of this photograph. The 15.20 Crewe to Swansea DMU is seen arriving at the station on 7th September 1989. (T.Heavyside)

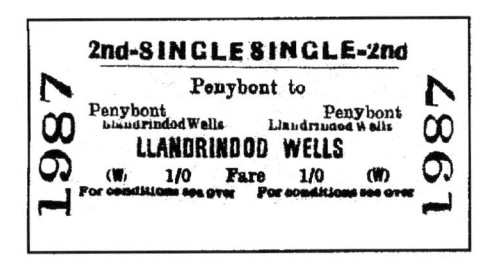

58. Looking south from the footbridge on the same occasion, another two car DMU arrives with the 15.28 Swansea to Crewe service. The signal box, which is now occupied by a small museum devoted to the railway, was originally situated to the north of the station as seen in photograph no.56. (T.Heavyside)

59. Since the marketing of the Central Wales route as the "Heart of Wales Line" following privatisation, a number of improvements to the station have taken place. Two class 153 DMUs were recorded passing at the rejuvenated station on 16th August 1996. (A.C.Mott)

60. Former LMS 4-6-0 no. 45407 and BR 2-6-0 no. 76079 are viewed as they arrived at the station prior to taking water from a fire hydrant on the down platform. The reinstated loop on the up side is clearly visible, whilst the scene is now dominated by a supermarket building which is completely out of character in the Victorian Spa town and is seen on 19th April 2008. (Mrs.B.Organ)

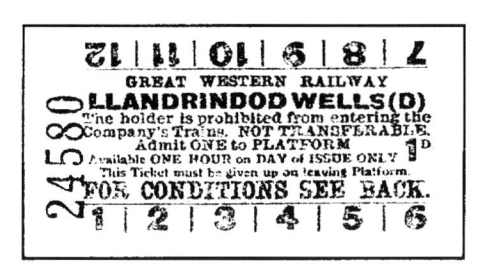

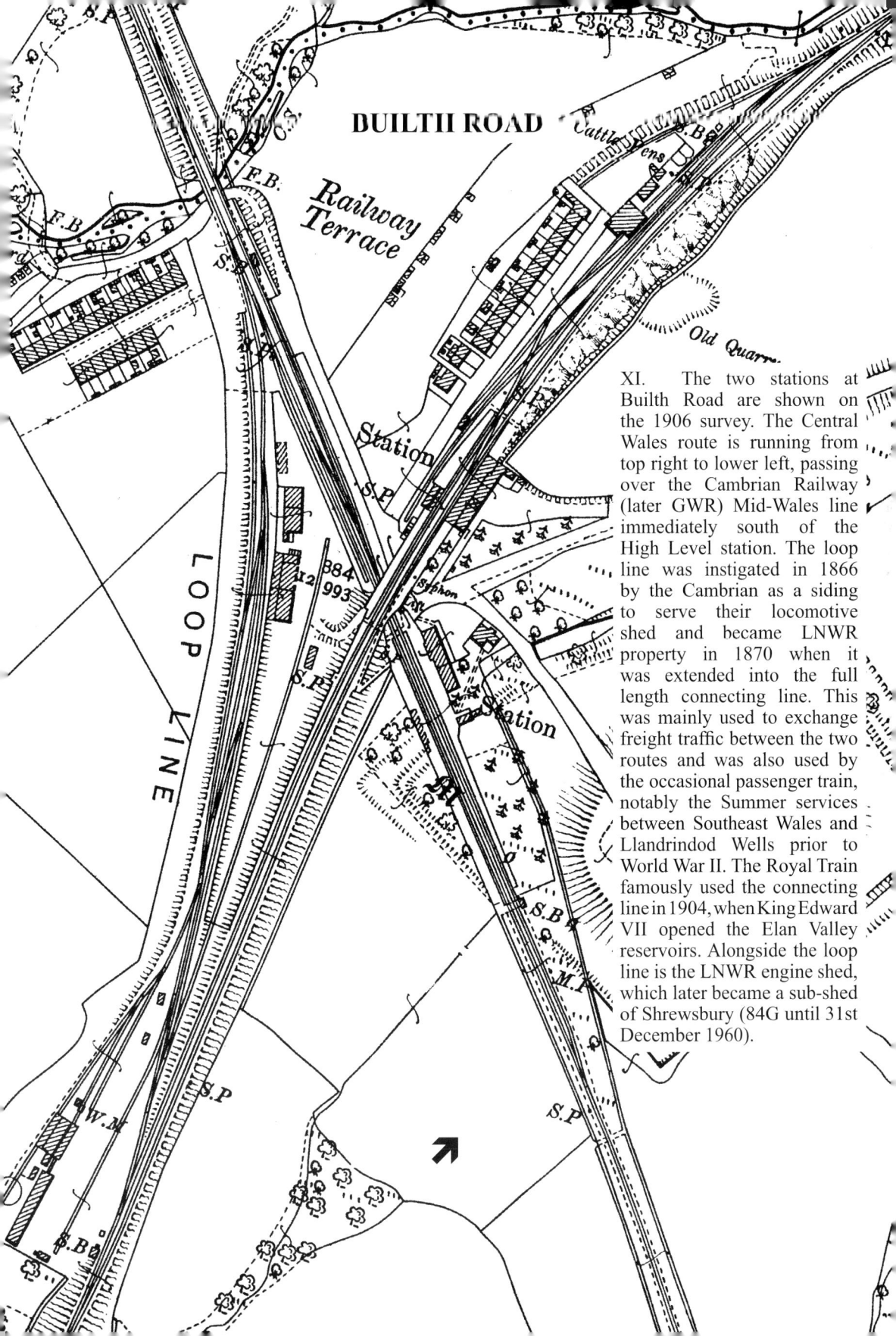

XI. The two stations at Builth Road are shown on the 1906 survey. The Central Wales route is running from top right to lower left, passing over the Cambrian Railway (later GWR) Mid-Wales line immediately south of the High Level station. The loop line was instigated in 1866 by the Cambrian as a siding to serve their locomotive shed and became LNWR property in 1870 when it was extended into the full length connecting line. This was mainly used to exchange freight traffic between the two routes and was also used by the occasional passenger train, notably the Summer services between Southeast Wales and Llandrindod Wells prior to World War II. The Royal Train famously used the connecting line in 1904, when King Edward VII opened the Elan Valley reservoirs. Alongside the loop line is the LNWR engine shed, which later became a sub-shed of Shrewsbury (84G until 31st December 1960).

61. South of Llandrindod Wells, the single track extended for seven miles until the northern approach to the High Level Station at the next major location, 38 miles from Craven Arms. Here was established the principal junction of the Central Wales Line, where it crossed the Mid-Wales Line. Former LNWR 0-8-0 no. 9358 was viewed at the south end of the station at the head of a freight train bound for Llandovery. This scene was recorded on 15th September 1949. (T.J.Edgington)

62. A Swansea bound freight train, hauled by 8F 2-8-0 no. 48525, is seen crossing the GWR line immediately to the south of the station, whilst a northbound passenger train can be seen in the up platform on 12th July 1956. (H.C.Casserley)

63. This view shows both ramps leading to Builth Road Low Level station. The GWR station building is prominent on the Mid-Wales Line down platform, whilst the structure behind the lower quadrant signal was a luggage hoist for transferring items between the two stations. This delightful scene was captured in 1956, six years before the former GWR route was closed. (H.C.Casserley)

64. This photograph of the north end of the High Level station was taken from the goods yard beyond the up platform. A northbound train is standing in the station whilst transferring passengers on 12th July 1956. (H.C.Casserley)

65. A few minutes later Fowler 2-6-4T no. 42307 was photographed as it departed from the station with the 6.05am service from Llandovery to Craven Arms. (H.C.Casserley)

66. Situated alongside the loop line that connected the two routes, the former LNWR engine shed was also used by the GWR. Former Midland Railway 0-6-0 no. 58213 is seen outside the single road shed on 12th July 1956. (H.C.Casserley)

67. Stanier 8F 2-8-0 no. 48347 arrives with a northbound freight train on 15th July 1957. Until the cessation of freight traffic over the Central Wales Line in 1964, the two principal commodities carried were coal from the south, whilst agricultural produce and livestock were generated from the north. In addition a long-lived service was the nightly "Burton Beer Train", which departed from Burton-on-Trent at 9.15pm and arrived at Swansea at 8.53am the following morning. The returning empty stock left Swansea at 8.45pm. (T.J.Edgington)

68. Class 5MT no. 44835 departs from the north end of the station at the head of the 10.35am Swansea to Shrewsbury train on the same occasion. The High Level and Low Level suffixes were instigated in 1950. Although Builth Road Low Level (named Llechryd until 1889) closed in 1962, the High Level suffix survived until 5th May 1968. "HALT" was added for a further 12 months. (T.J.Edgington)

69. This view of the north end of the complex, looking south, shows the station still in its most complete form. The bay platform and headshunt alongside the up platform, were photographed on 16th April 1960. (J.C.Gillham)

70. This view of the southern end of Builth Road High Level on the same day shows the large station building on the down platform. Also visible is the small wooden shelter on the up platform and the goods shed in the distance. (J.C.Gillham)

71. Viewed from the same location, 2-6-4T no. 42388 was recorded whilst it was about to depart from the down platform with the 7.40am train from Craven Arms to Swansea on 18th March 1961. The bay windows allowed the station master to survey the site. (R.Patterson)

BRITISH RAILWAYS (W)
THE RAILWAY EXECUTIVE.
PARKING TICKET FOR
MOTOR CYCLE
at BUILTH ROAD H.L.
Registration No..................
FEE 6d. Z
Available on Day of issue only.
FOR CONDITIONS SEE BACK

045   045

72. During the final year of the former GWR presence at this important junction, Ivatt Class 2MT 2-6-0 no. 46401 was recorded at the engine shed prior to hauling a train along the Mid-Wales Line on 15th April 1962. This site is now occupied by a timber yard, to which road access is made via the old GWR track bed. (R.Patterson)

73. Class 8F 2-8-0 no. 48470 takes water whilst hauling a southbound freight train. The station porter is seen hauling a large consignment on his trolley in the foreground, whilst another member of the station staff and a passenger are doubtless discussing the imminent closure of the Mid-Wales Line. This scene was captured on 13th November 1962, five weeks before the GWR line and the Low Level station was lost. (P.Chancellor)

74. Viewed from the platform extension, which was constructed on the bridge over the GWR line, class 5MT 4-6-0 no. 45190 was recorded as it replenished its water supply before proceeding to Swansea at 1.40pm on 2nd August 1963. (E.Wilmshurst)

Builth Road Low Level is featured in the *Brecon to Newtown* album.

75. Seven years later the line had been singled and the up platform buildings demolished. Today, although the station remains open, the awning has been removed and the goods shed is now in use as a council depot. This view of the once bustling station was recorded on 21st June 1970. (E.Wilmshurst)

SOUTH OF BUILTH ROAD

76. A short distance to the south of the station, the Central Wales Line crosses the River Wye by this two span iron bridge. This structure, which also marked the former boundary between Radnorshire and Breconshire, was photographed around 1909. (G.Perkins/R.Carpenter coll.)

CILMERI

77.   Opened 11th March 1867 as Cefn-y-bedd, it aquired the name of Cilmery in the following year (Halt between 1936 and 1969) and Cilmeri on 12th May 1980. After leaving Builth Road, the line became single again. Shortly after crossing the River Wye, a gradient of 1 in 80 is ascended via two short tunnels for almost two miles to Cilmery Halt, where 8F 2-8-0 no. 48470 was recorded hauling a southbound freight train on 15th June 1963. (R.Patterson)

GARTH (POWYS)

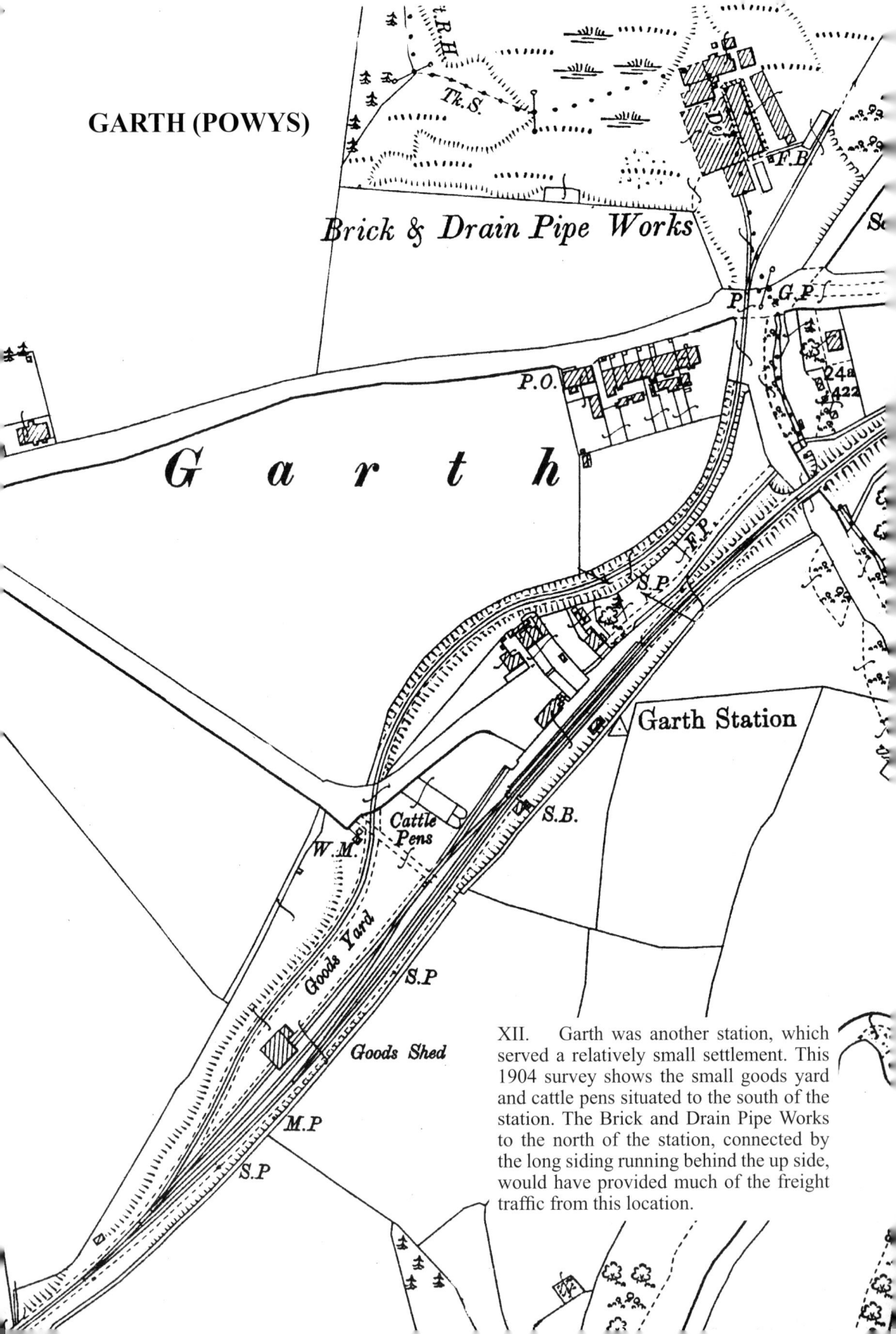

XII. Garth was another station, which served a relatively small settlement. This 1904 survey shows the small goods yard and cattle pens situated to the south of the station. The Brick and Drain Pipe Works to the north of the station, connected by the long siding running behind the up side, would have provided much of the freight traffic from this location.

78. Located 43 miles from Craven Arms, this was the next station with a passing loop. Class 5MT no. 73034 is pictured as it halted briefly at the station whilst hauling the 2.40pm Shrewsbury to Swansea train on 27th April 1963. (R.Patterson)

79. Two months later and how the grass on the embankment has grown, it was probably a wet Spring! On this occasion, class 4MT 2-6-4T no. 80099 was in charge of the 2.40pm from Shrewsbury when viewed on 15th June 1963. (R.Patterson)

LLANGAMMARCH

80. Following a two-mile long undulating section, which includes a short tunnel 55 yards in length, this is the next station on the route. It includes a small goods yard behind the building. This view looking northeast towards Builth Road is from 16th July 1959. (R.M.Casserley)

LLANWRTYD

XIII. The station, shown on this 1905 survey, is situated about a quarter of a mile from the town centre. Its political status allows it to describe itself as a town and as such it claims to be the smallest in Britain. The station has retained both platforms and the passing loop, whilst the goods shed has also survived although not connected by rail.

81. Four miles beyond Llangammarch Wells, on a section that includes the longest level stretch of track on the entire route, the next principal station is approached. Situated 48 miles from Craven Arms, this attractive station had a passing loop, two platforms and freight facilities to the north of the complex. This scene, looking northeast, was recorded on 15th June 1963. (R.Patterson)

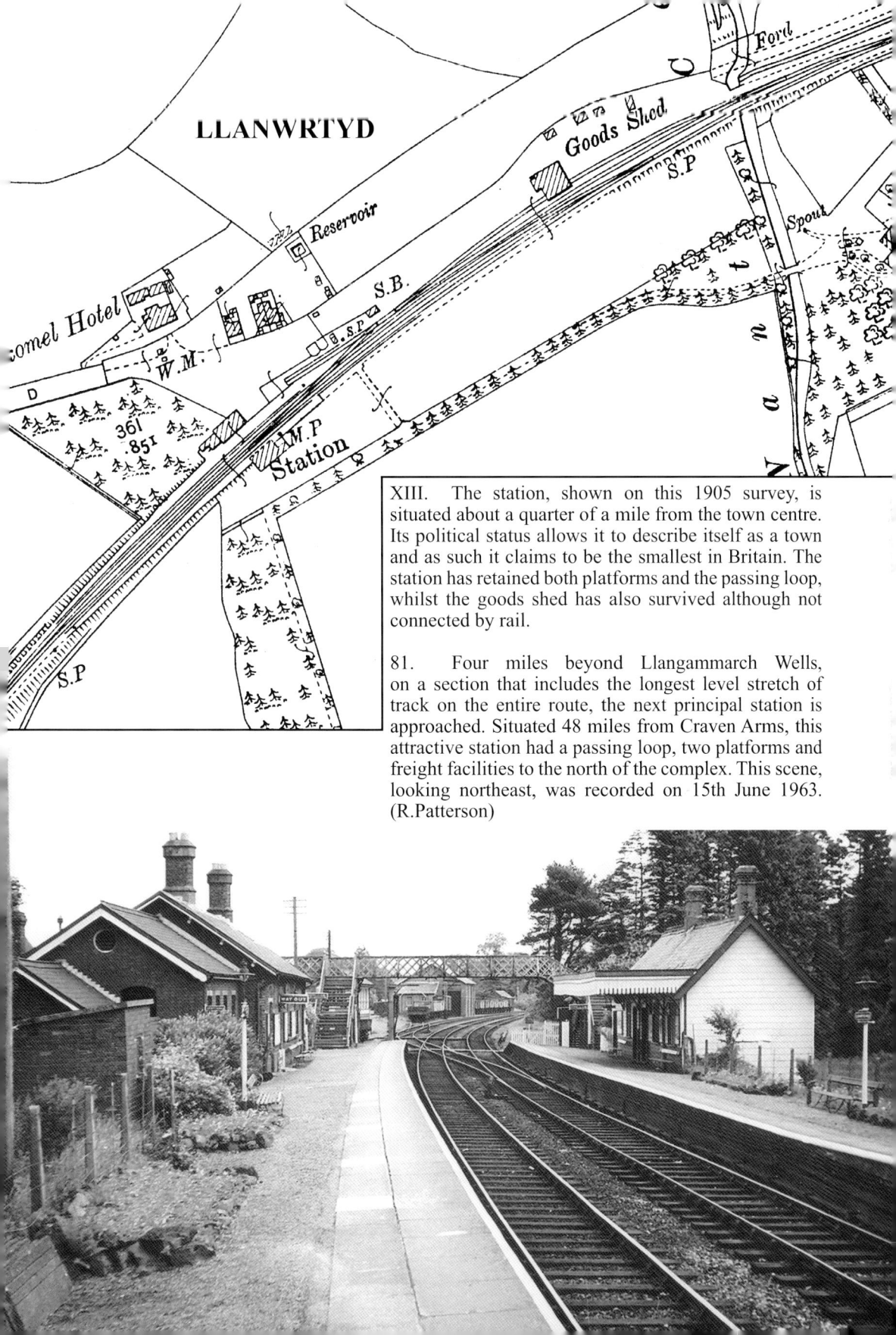

82. The station was viewed looking southwest, whilst a northbound ballast train approached the up platform on 16th June 1963. The excellent condition of the permanent way is evident in this scene. (R.Patterson)

83. A few minutes later the ballast train, hauled by 2-8-0 no. 48307, was pictured from the footbridge as it arrived at the station. (R.Patterson)

84. A later view of Llanwrtyd was recorded when a three car DMU departed to the north with the 12.27pm Swansea to Shrewsbury service on 14th June 1983. The signal box was closed in 1986, however the goods shed survived and is now in private industrial use. (T.Heavyside)

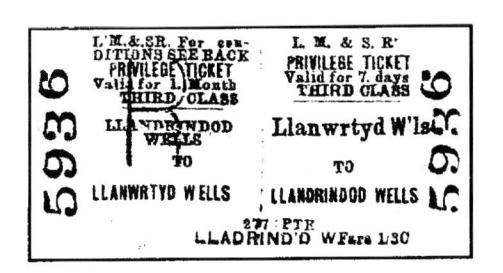

85. Our final view of this pleasant location shows the same three car DMU seen in the previous photograph. The northbound train was recorded as it arrived at the up platform in June 1983. (T.Heavyside)

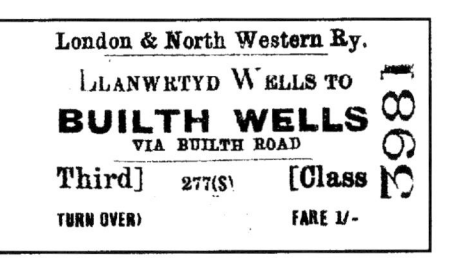

London & North Western Ry.
LLANWRTYD WELLS TO
BUILTH WELLS
VIA BUILTH ROAD
Third]   277(S)   [Class
TURN OVER)   FARE 1/-

NORTH OF SUGAR LOAF

86.   Class 8F 2-8-0 no. 48309 was recorded as it drifted down the 1 in 80 gradient towards Llanwrtyd Wells, with the foothills of the Mynydd Mallaen in the background, whilst hauling a northbound freight train on 9th June 1953. (D.K.Jones coll.)

87.   The 11.45am Shrewsbury to Swansea service, hauled by class 5MT 4-6-0 no. 73025, storms up the final stretch of 1 in 80 gradient towards Sugar Loaf Summit, 51 miles from Craven Arms, on 15th June 1963. (R.Patterson)

SUGAR LOAF

88. A pre-grouping view looking north, shows the original wooden construction of the platforms at this isolated location, opened as Sugar Loaf Summit in 1899 as a staff halt with occasional public usage. Note that the actual summit is adjacent to the southern end of the platforms. (Lens of Sutton coll.)

89. A later view of the summit station features the distinctive signal box and the passing loop. Visible above the embankment are the two cottages, which were occupied by railway employees, notably the signalmen. This scene, looking north, was photographed on 6th July 1958. (R.M.Casserley)

90. A more detailed view of the LNWR signal box was captured from a southbound train, under the scrutiny of the signalman standing on the steps of the box on 12th July 1956. (H.C.Casserley)

91. The northern portal of the single line Sugar Loaf Tunnel, situated on the 1 in 70 descent from the summit can be seen in the distance. Also visible are the points at the end of the passing loop and the siding with its sand drag in front of the permanent way hut. This view, looking in a southerly direction, was taken on 6th July 1958. (H.C.Casserley)

92. Since 1965, the loop has been removed and the signal box demolished. All that now remains is the up platform renamed Sugar Loaf in 1989, whilst hauling a steam hauled special towards South Wales, class 5MT no. 44767 paused for a "photo stop" at the summit on 23rd May 1993. (D.Trevor Rowe)

SOUTH OF SUGAR LOAF

93.   After passing down long sweeping curves for four miles, the line crosses the 283 yard long Cynghordy Viaduct, which is the largest on the Central Wales route. The curved 17 arch structure was viewed from the south on 6th July 1958. (H.C.Casserley)

94. A more detailed study of the viaduct was obtained as a southbound DMU crossed the sandstone and brick structure with the 10.50am Shrewsbury to Swansea service on 14th June 1983. (T.Heavyside)

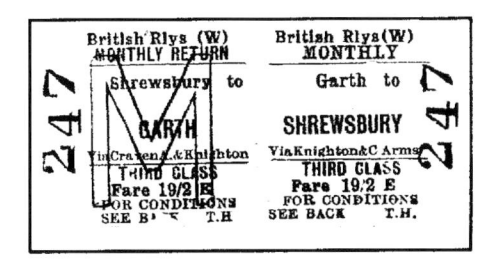

CYNGHORDY

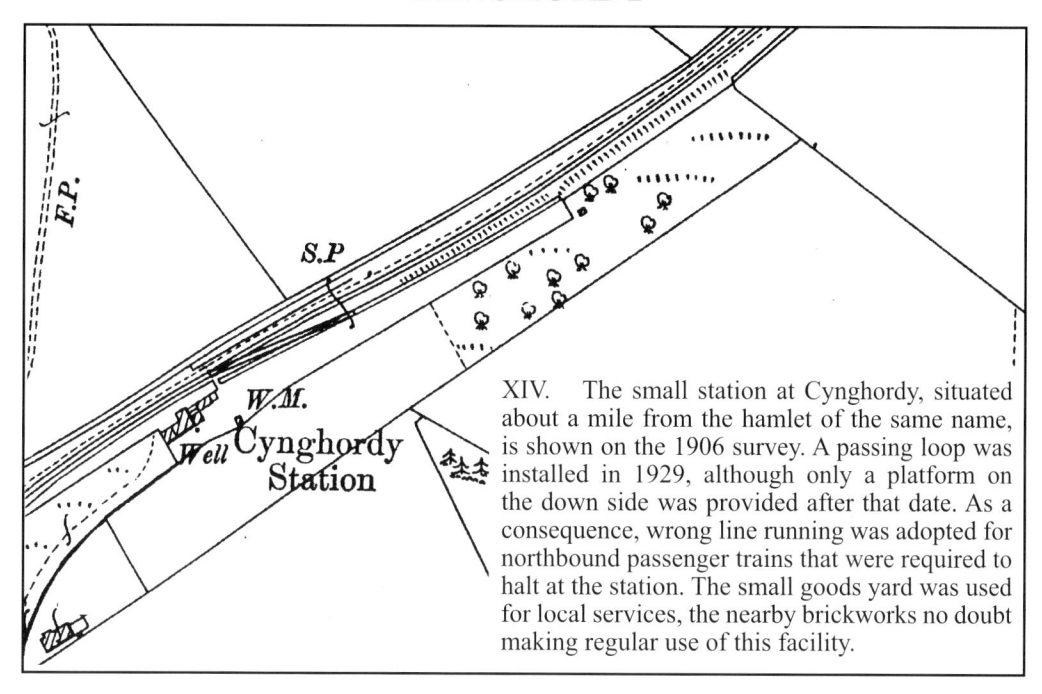

XIV. The small station at Cynghordy, situated about a mile from the hamlet of the same name, is shown on the 1906 survey. A passing loop was installed in 1929, although only a platform on the down side was provided after that date. As a consequence, wrong line running was adopted for northbound passenger trains that were required to halt at the station. The small goods yard was used for local services, the nearby brickworks no doubt making regular use of this facility.

95. Wrong line running! The up "York Mail", hauled by 4-6-0 no.45406 was recorded arriving at the down platform, whilst a southbound train waits in the passing loop on the up side. This scene was recorded on 12th July 1956. (H.C.Casserley)

96. A panoramic view of the station looking south was obtained from the signal box on 6th July 1958. The buffer stops of the small goods siding can be seen in the foreground. (H.C.Casserley)

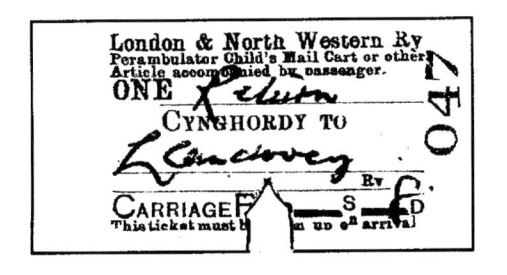

97. The station building with its gable ended office, which originally contained the signal box, was also recorded on the same date. One wonders if the fire buckets were ever used for their intended purpose. (R.M.Casserley)

98. A closer view of the signal box was photographed from the north end of the platform on 6th July 1958. The wooden construction of these buildings was very much in keeping with their surroundings. (H.C.Casserley)

99. The characteristic LMS signal box that controlled the passing loop, after it was installed in 1929, also features in this view looking north on 16th June 1963. The Ford Van seen behind the station must have been almost new! (R.Patterson)

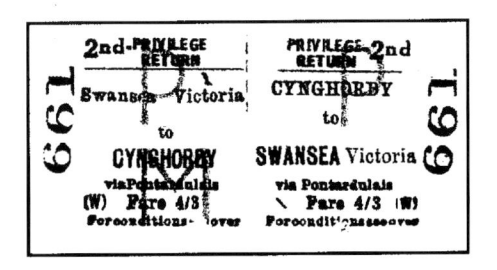

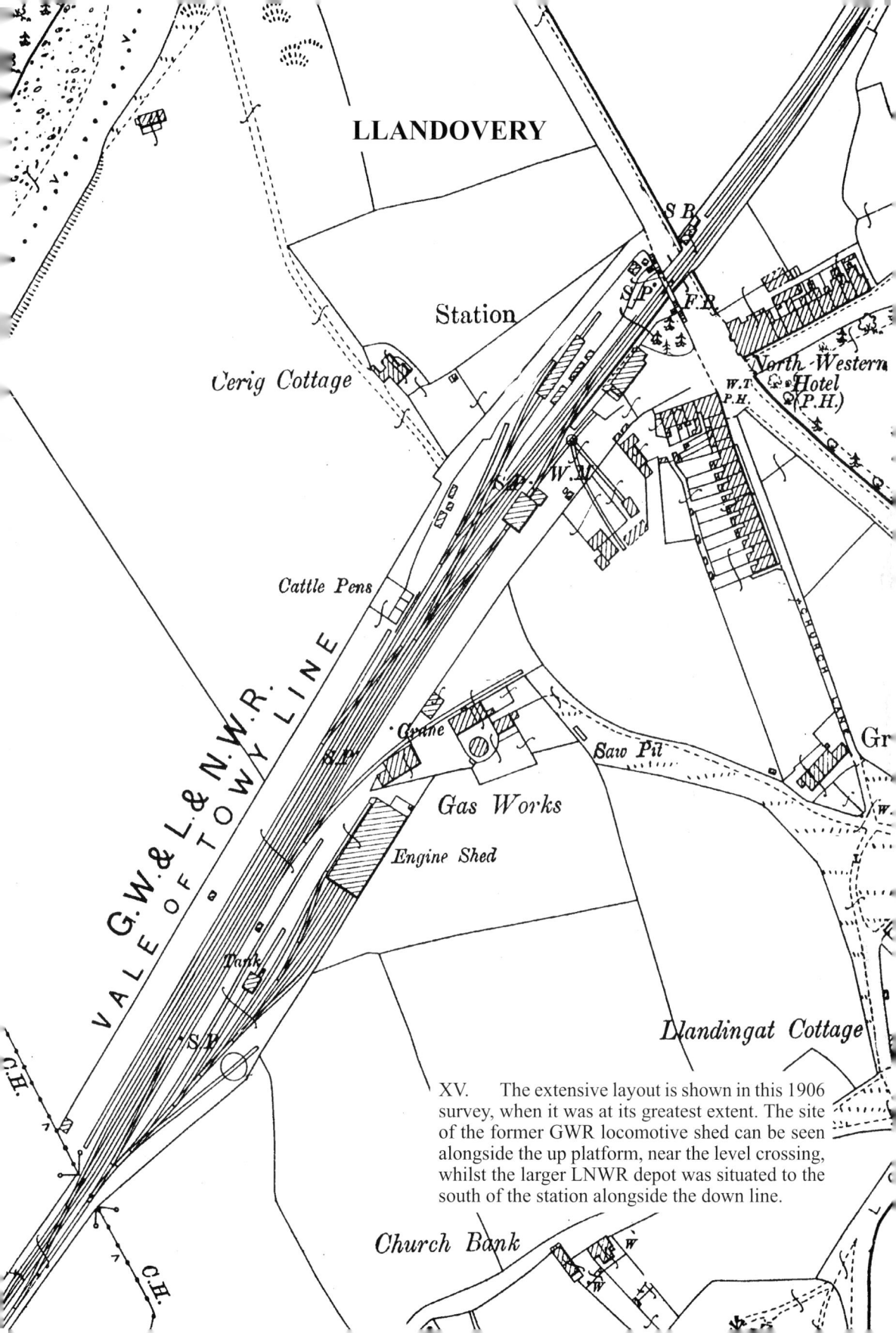

LLANDOVERY

Cerig Cottage

Station

North Western Hotel (P.H.)

G.W. & L.&N.W.R.
VALE OF TOWY LINE

Cattle Pens

Crane

Saw Pit

Gas Works

Engine Shed

Tank

Llandingat Cottage

XV. The extensive layout is shown in this 1906 survey, when it was at its greatest extent. The site of the former GWR locomotive shed can be seen alongside the up platform, near the level crossing, whilst the larger LNWR depot was situated to the south of the station alongside the down line.

Church Bank

100. Class 5MT 4-6-0 no. 45190 arrives with the 12.30pm Swansea to Shrewsbury service on 15th September 1949. The area behind the small platform building was once the site of the GWR locomotive shed, which was replaced by the LNWR depot during the early 20th century. (T.J.Edgington)

101. The fireman of Fowler class 4MT 2-6-4T, no. 42390, hands over the token to the signalman at Llandovery No.1 box on the northern approach to the station whilst hauling the heavy 6.25am Shrewsbury to Swansea service on 8th September 1951. (H.C.Casserley)

102. A few minutes later, no. 42305 was recorded northbound as it passed the level crossing at the north end of the station. The quiet road which the railway is seen crossing is in fact the A40 trunk route to Southwest Wales! Llandovery is located 59 miles from Central Wales Junction at Craven Arms. (H.C.Casserley)

103. The large four road locomotive depot was situated to the south of the station. Although this section of the Central Wales Line was jointly owned by the LNWR (LMS) and GWR, the motive power based at the depot was distinctly of Crewe and Derby origin. This view is also from 8th September 1951. (H.C.Casserley)

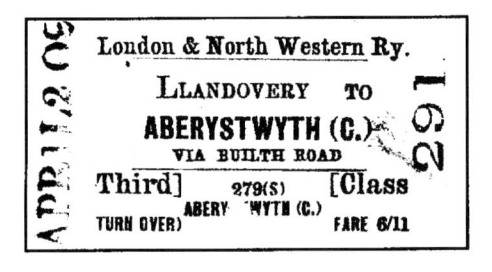

104. Former LNWR 0-8-0 no. 49138 was captured alongside the up platform whilst working a northbound freight on the same occasion. This was one of the Class G1 locomotives that were rebuilt in 1936 with Belpaire boilers to become Class G2a, increasing their classification from 6F to 7F. (R.M.Casserley)

105. The exterior of the station is seen from the North Western Hotel on 13th July 1956. Llandovery was, and indeed still is, an important agricultural and livestock market town, which generated much valuable traffic to the Central Wales Line prior to the cessation of freight trains on the route. (H.C.Casserley)

106. Inspection saloon no. M15807M was built at Wolverton Works in 1909 as a Third Class Dining Carriage. It was recorded in the goods yard on 12th July 1956, six months before it was withdrawn from service. (H.C.Casserley)

107. This view is from the up platform on 6th July 1958. The main station buildings are seen on the down side with the North Western Hotel in the background. (R.M.Casserley)

108. Class 8F 2-8-0 no. 48732 was recorded in the extensive goods yard at this important location with a freight train bound for South Wales in 1965. (D.K.Jones coll.)

109. By the time that this view was obtained, the awnings on the down platform buildings had been removed along with much of the other infrastructure. A three-car DMU was recorded as it drew into the station with the 10.49am departure from Shrewsbury to Swansea on 2nd October 1982. (E.Wilmshurst)

110. On the same occasion, another DMU was viewed as it waited in the up platform of the now reduced station complex with the 12.25pm service from Swansea to Shrewsbury via Llanelli. (E.Wilmshurst)

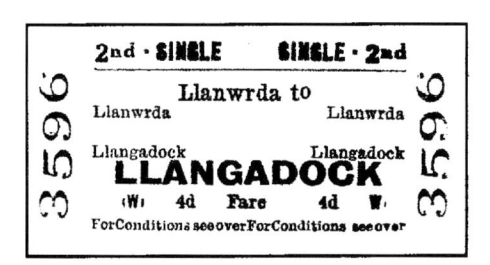

2nd · SINGLE	SINGLE · 2nd
Llanwrda to	
Llanwrda	Llanwrda
Llangadock	Llangadock
LLANGADOCK	
(W) 4d Fare	4d W
ForConditions see over	ForConditions see over

35596 35596

LLANWRDA

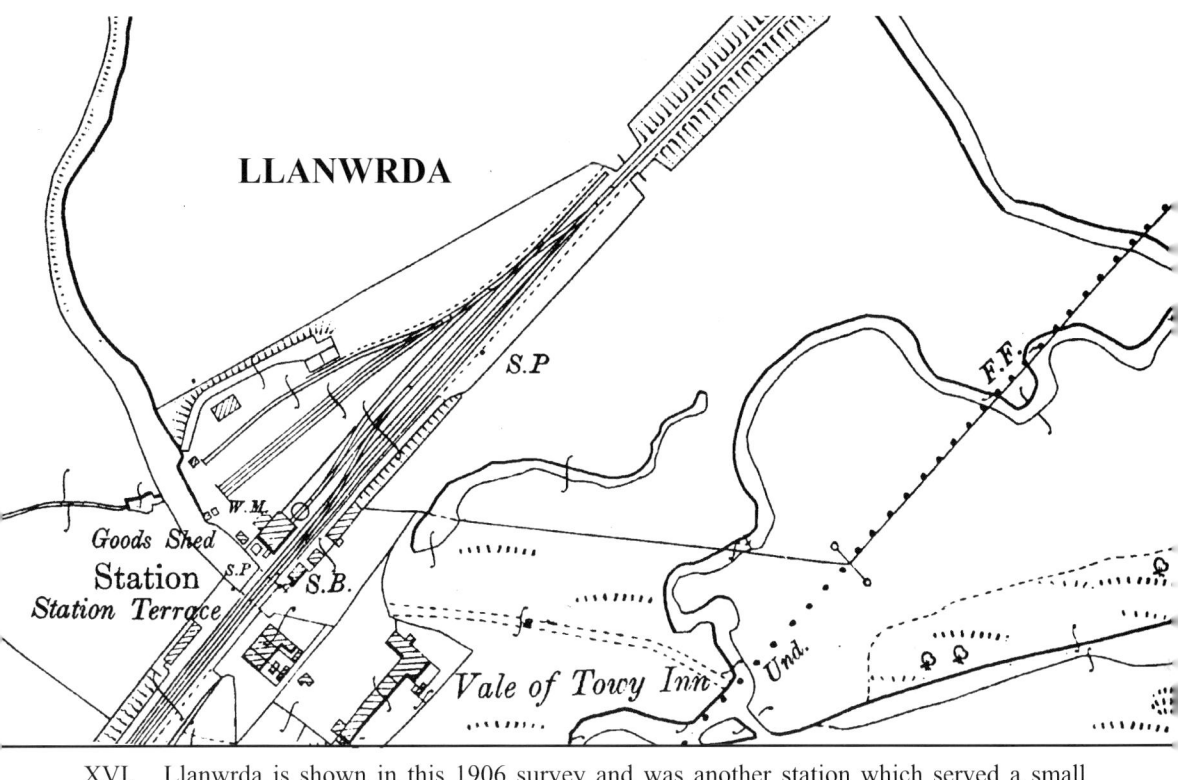

XVI. Llanwrda is shown in this 1906 survey and was another station which served a small community. The station was named Lampeter Road until 1868. The goods yard was mainly used for agricultural purposes.

111. The photographer's familiar Hillman 10 was seen alongside a number of other period cars on the station approach on 7th July 1958. The term HALT was applied in 1965-69.
(H.C.Casserley)

112. On the same occasion, class 5MT 4-6-0 no. 45143 was recorded arriving at the station whilst hauling the 12.00pm departure from Shrewsbury to Swansea train. Situated 63 miles from Craven Arms, the attractive station boasted a small goods shed and yard alongside the passing loop on the up side. (H.C.Casserley)

113. This view of the downgraded complex was recorded on 16th June 1963 and the station is still open despite the absence of track serving the down platform. (R.Patterson)

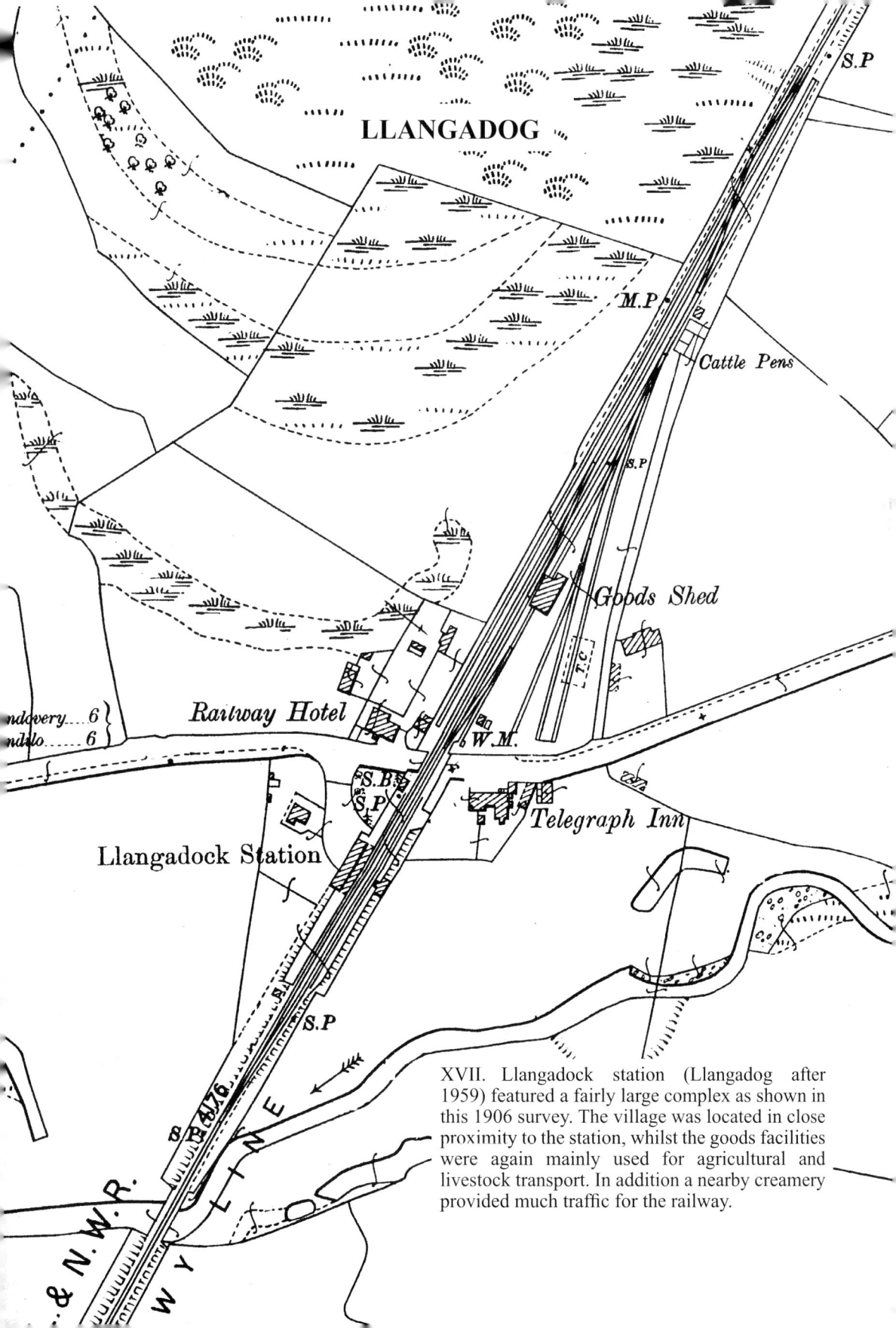

XVII. Llangadock station (Llangadog after 1959) featured a fairly large complex as shown in this 1906 survey. The village was located in close proximity to the station, whilst the goods facilities were again mainly used for agricultural and livestock transport. In addition a nearby creamery provided much traffic for the railway.

114. The GWR influence in the station architecture was beginning to become apparent on the former Vale of Towy Railway section of the route, as shown in this south facing view of 7th July 1958. (H.C.Casserley)

115. A view in the opposite direction, towards Llandovery, shows the GWR style of the station to full advantage. Note that the name board had been changed to the Welsh spelling by the time that this photograph was taken on 15th June 1963. (R.Patterson)

GLANRHYD HALT

116. Situated 66 miles from the start of our journey, this small single road station was located a short distance west of the bridge over the River Towy. The station closed on 20th July 1931 and reopened as a halt on 19th December 1938, finally closing on 7th March 1955. This view north is from 16th June 1963. (R.Patterson)

Talley Road was a simple unphotogenic platform, a little over one mile from Llandilo. It became a halt in 1941 and closed on 4th April 1955.

LLANDEILO

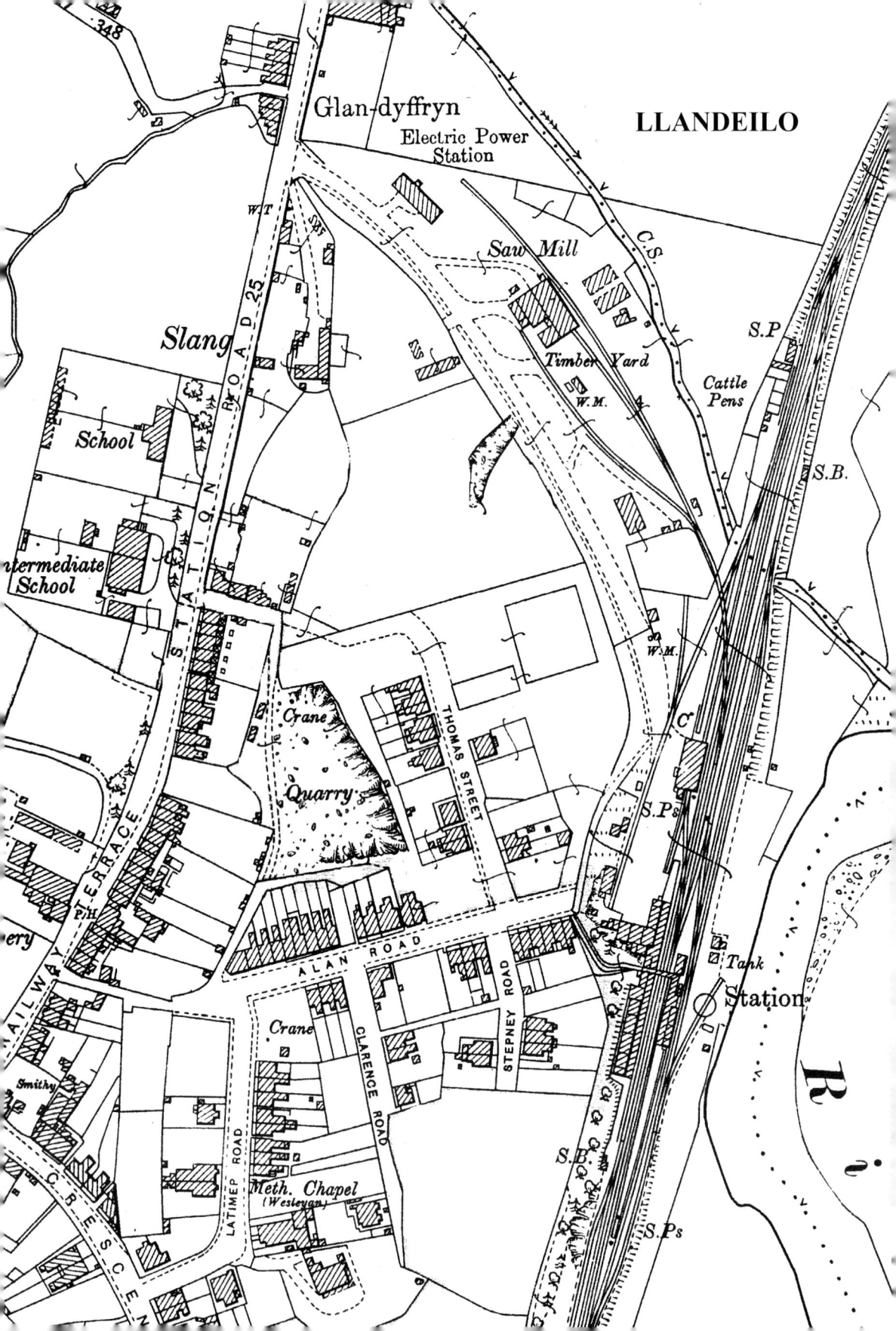

Glan-dyffryn
Electric Power Station

Saw Mill

Slang

School

Timber Yard

C.S.

S.P.

Cattle Pens

S.B.

Intermediate School

W.M.

STATION ROAD 25

Crane

Quarry

THOMAS STREET

W.M.

RAILWAY TERRACE

P.H.

S.Ps

ALAN ROAD

Crane

CLARENCE ROAD

STEPNEY ROAD

LATIMER ROAD

Tank

Station

Smithy

CRESCENT

Meth. Chapel
(Wesleyan)

S.B.

S.Ps

R i

← XVIII. Llandilo, as it was originally named, was a very extensive station, even boasting a refreshment room during its heyday. This 1906 survey shows the timber yard to the north of the station, which had its own rail connection and provided much valuable freight traffic. The bay platform on the down side of the station was used by trains from the Carmarthen branch, the junction for which was situated just beyond the bottom of this map. All that now remains of this once grand complex are the two platforms and the rarely used passing loop on the down side, with only the up platform being normally in use.

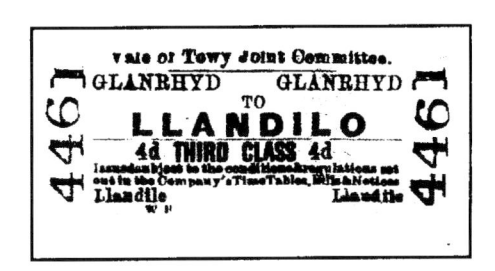

117. The austere modern signal box, built by British Railways in 1955, stands at the north end of the down platform. Located 70 miles from Craven Arms, this was the largest intermediate station on the Central Wales Line. Apart from the replacement signal box, the station architecture was still very much typical of the GWR when it was photographed on 30th April 1960. (R.Patterson)

PASSENGERS ARE
REQUESTED TO CROSS THE
LINE BY THE BRIDGE
BOOKING OFFICE
42385

LLANDILO
JUNCTION FOR
CARMARTHEN LINE
73090

← 118. Although we were now in former GWR territory, the majority of locomotives were still mainly of LMS origin, 12 years after nationalisation and the transfer of the line to BR Western Region control. Fowler 2-6-4T no. 42385 was recorded as it arrived at the up platform whilst hauling the 6.15am Swansea to Shrewsbury service on 30th April 1960. These venerable Derby built locomotives were soon to be displaced by the BR variants of class 4MT 2-6-4Ts. (R.Patterson)

← 119. Class 5MT 4-6-0 no. 73090 has arrived at the down platform with the "York Mail" from York to Swansea at 7.15 am on 18th March 1961. The train had left York at 9.50pm the previous evening. (E.Wilmshurst)

120. A view to the north over 30 years later shows how this once magnificent station had been reduced in status. A type 153 single car unit was recorded as it passed the closed and since demolished station buildings and signal box whilst working a southbound service to Swansea, via Llanelli, on 29th August 1992. Note the two levels of the up platform, which is a legacy of the Vale of Towy Railway. The name was changed from the traditional name of Llandilo in 1971, during the period that many other Welsh towns were controversially renamed. (E.Wilmshurst)

MP Middleton Press

EVOLVING THE ULTIMATE RAIL ENCYCLOPEDIA

Easebourne Lane, Midhurst, West Sussex.
GU29 9AZ Tel:01730 813169

www.middletonpress.co.uk email:info@middletonpress.co.uk

A-978 0 906520 B- 978 1 873793 C- 978 1 901706 D-978 1 904474 E - 978 1 906008

OOP Out of print at time of printing - Please check availability BROCHURE AVAILABLE SHOWING NEW TITLES

A
Abergavenny to Merthyr C 91 8
Abertillery and Ebbw Vale Lines D 84 5
Aldgate & Stepney Tramways B 70 1
Allhallows - Branch Line to A 62 8
Alton - Branch Lines to A 11 6
Andover to Southampton A 82 6
Ascot - Branch Lines around A 64 2
Ashburton - Branch Line to B 95 4
Ashford - Steam to Eurostar B 67 1
Ashford to Dover A 48 2
Austrian Narrow Gauge D 04 3
Avonmouth - BL around D 42 5
Aylesbury to Rugby D 91 3
B
Baker Street to Uxbridge D 90 6
Banbury to Birmingham D 27 2
Barking to Southend C 80 2
Barnet & Finchley Tramways B 93 0
Barry - Branch Lines around D 50 0
Bath Green Park to Bristol C 36 9
Bath to Evercreech Junction A 60 4
Bath Tramways B 86 2
Battle over Portsmouth 1940 A 29 1
Battle over Sussex 1940 A 79 6
Bedford to Wellingborough D 31 9
Betwixt Petersfield & Midhurst A 94 9
Birmingham to Wolverhampton E 25 3
Birmingham Trolleybuses E 19 2
Blackpool Tramways 1933-66
Bletchley to Cambridge D 94 4
Bletchley to Rugby E 07 9
Blitz over Sussex 1941-42 B 35 0
Bodmin - Branch Lines around B 83 1
Bognor at War 1939-45 B 59 6
Bombers over Sussex 1943-45 B 51 0
Bournemouth & Poole Trys B 47 3
Bournemouth to Evercreech Jn A 46 8
Bournemouth to Weymouth A 57 4
Bournemouth Trolleybuses C 10 9
Bradford Trolleybuses D 19 7
Brecon to Neath D 43 2
Brecon to Newport D 16 6
Brecon to Newtown E 06 2
Brighton to Eastbourne A 16 1
Brighton to Worthing A 03 1
Brighton Trolleybuses D 34 0
Bristols Tramways B 57 2
Bristol to Taunton D 03 6
Bromley South to Rochester B 23 7
Bromsgrove to Birmingham D 87 6
Bromsgrove to Gloucester D 73 9
Brunel - A railtour of his achievements D 74 6
Bude - Branch Line to B 29 9
Burnham to Evercreech Jn A 68 0
Burton & Ashby Tramways C 51 2
C
Camberwell & West Norwood Tys B 22 0
Cambridge to Ely D 55 5
Canterbury - Branch Lines around B 58 9
Cardiff Trolleybuses D 64 7
Caterham & Tattenham Corner B 25 1
Changing Midhurst C 15 4
Chard and Yeovil - BLs around C 30 7
Charing Cross to Dartford A 75 8
Charing Cross to Orpington A 96 3
Cheddar - Branch Line to B 90 9
Cheltenham to Andover C 43 7
Cheltenham to Redditch D 81 4
Chesterfield Tramways D 37 1
Chesterfield Trolleybuses D 51 7
Chester Tramways E 04 8
Chichester to Portsmouth A 14 7
Clapham & Streatham Trys B 97 8
Clapham Junction to Beckenham Jn B 36 7
Cleobury Mortimer - BLs around E 18 5
Clevedon & Portishead - BLs to D 18 0
Collectors Trains, Trolleys & Trams D 29 6
Colonel Stephens D62 3
Cornwall Narrow Gauge D 56 2
Cowdray & Easebourne D 96 8
Craven Arms to Wellington
Crawley to Littlehampton A 34 5
Cromer - Branch Lines around C 26 0
Croydons Tramways B 42 8
Croydons Trolleybuses B 73 2
Croydon to East Grinstead B 48 0
Crystal Palace (HL) & Catford Loop A 87 1
Cyprus Narrow Gauge E13 0
D
Darlington - Leamside - Newcastle E 28 4
Darlington to Newcastle D 98 2
Darlington Trolleybuses D 33 3
Dartford to Sittingbourne B 34 3
Derby Tramways D 17 3
Derby Trolleybuses C 72 7
Derwent Valley - Branch Line to the D 06 7
Devon Narrow Gauge E 09 3
Didcot to Banbury D 02 9
Didcot to Swindon C 84 0
Didcot to Winchester C 13 0
Dorset & Somerset Narrow Gauge D 76 0
Douglas to Peel C 88 8
Douglas to Port Erin C 55 0
Douglas to Ramsey D 39 5
Dovers Tramways B 24 4
Dover to Ramsgate A 78 9
Dublin Northwards in the 1950s
Dunstable - Branch Lines to E 27 7
E
Ealing to Slough C 42 0
East Cornwall Mineral Railways D 22 7
East Croydon to Three Bridges A 53 6
East Grinstead - Branch Lines to A 07 9
East Ham & West Ham Tramways B 52 7
East London - Branch Lines of C 44 4
East London Line B 80 0
East Ridings Secret Resistance D 21 0
Edgware & Willesden Tramways C 18 5
Effingham Junction - BLs around A 74 1
Ely to Norwich C 90 1
Embankment & Waterloo Tramways B 41 1
Enfield Town & Palace Gates - BL to D 32 6
Epsom to Horsham A 30 7
Euston to Harrow & Wealdstone C 89 5
Exeter & Taunton Tramways B 32 9
Exeter to Barnstaple B 15 2
Exeter to Newton Abbot C 49 9
Exeter to Tavistock B 69 5
Exmouth - Branch Lines to B 00 8
F
Fairford - Branch Line to A 52 9
Falmouth, Helston & St. Ives - BL to C 74 1
Fareham to Salisbury A 67 3
Faversham to Dover B 05 3
Felixstowe & Aldeburgh - BL to D 20 3
Fenchurch Street to Barking C 20 8
Festiniog - 50 yrs of enterprise C 83 3
Festiniog 1946-55 E 01 7
Festiniog in the Fifties B 68 8
Festiniog in the Sixties B 91 6
Frome to Bristol B 77 0
Fulwell - Trams, Trolleys & Buses D 11 1
G
Gloucester to Bristol D 35 7
Gloucester to Cardiff D 66 1
Gosport & Horndean Trys B 92 3
Gosport - Branch Lines around A 36 9
Great Yarmouth Tramways D 13 5
Greece Narrow Gauge D 72 2
Grimsby & Cleethorpes Trolleybuses D 86 9
H
Hammersmith & Hounslow Trys C 33 8
Hampshire Narrow Gauge D 36 4
Hampstead & Highgate Tramways B 53 4
Harrow to Watford D 14 2
Hastings to Ashford A 37 6
Hastings Tramways B 18 3
Hawkhurst - Branch Line to A 66 6
Hay-on-Wye - Branch Lines around D 92 0
Hayling - Branch Line to A 12 3
Haywards Heath to Seaford A 28 4
Hemel Hempstead - Branch Lines to D 88 3
Henley, Windsor & Marlow - BL to C77 2
Hereford to Newport D 54 8
Hexham to Carlisle D 75 3
Hitchin to Peterborough D 07 4
Holborn & Finsbury Tramways B 79 4
Holborn Viaduct to Lewisham A 81 9
Horsham - Branch Lines to A 02 4
Huddersfield Tramways D 95 1
Huddersfield Trolleybuses C 92 5
Hull Tramways D60 9
Hull Trolleybuses D 24 1
Huntingdon - Branch Lines around A 93 2
I
Ilford & Barking Tramways B 61 9
Ilford to Shenfield C 97 0
Ilfracombe - Branch Line to B 21 3
Ilkeston & Glossop Tramways D 40 1
Index to Middleton Press Stations E 24 6
Industrial Rlys of the South East A 09 3
Ipswich to Saxmundham C 41 3
Ipswich Trolleybuses D 59 3
Isle of Wight Lines - 50 yrs C 12 3
K
Keighley Tramways & Trolleybuses D 83 8
Kent & East Sussex Waterways A 72 X
Kent Narrow Gauge C 45 1
Kent Seaways - Hoys to Hovercraft D 79 1
Kidderminster to Shrewsbury E10 9
Kingsbridge - Branch Line to C 98 7
Kingston & Hounslow Loops A 83 3
Kingston & Wimbledon Tramways B 56 5
Kingswear - Branch Line to C 17 8
L
Lambourn - Branch Line to C 70 3
Launceston & Princetown - BL to C 19 2
Lewisham to Dartford A 92 5
Lines around Wimbledon B 75 6
Liverpool Street to Chingford D 01 2
Liverpool Street to Ilford C 34 5
Liverpool Tramways - Eastern C 04 8
Liverpool Tramways - Northern C 46 8
Liverpool Tramways - Southern C 23 9
Llandudno & Colwyn Bay Tramways E 17 8
London Bridge to Addiscombe B 20 6
London Bridge to East Croydon A 58 1
London Termini - Past and Proposed D 00 5
London to Portsmouth Waterways B 43 5
Longmoor - Branch Lines to A 41 3
Looe - Branch Line to C 22 2
Ludlow to Hereford E 14 7
Lydney - Branch Lines around E 26 0
Lyme Regis - Branch Line to A 45 1
Lynton - Branch Line to B 04 6
M
Maidstone & Chatham Tramways B 40 4
March - Branch Lines around B 09 1
Margate & Ramsgate Tramways C 52 9
Marylebone to Rickmansworth D49 4
Melton Constable to Yarmouth Beach E 03 1
Midhurst - Branch Lines around A 49 9
Military Defence of West Sussex A 23 9
Military Signals, South Coast C 54 3
Mitcham Junction Lines B 01 5
Mitchell & company C 59 8
Monmouth - Branch Lines to E 20 8
Monmouthshire Eastern Valleys D 71 5
Moreton-in-Marsh to Worcester D 26 5
Moretonhampstead - BL to C 27 7
Mountain Ash to Neath D 80 7
N
Newbury to Westbury C 66 6
Newcastle to Hexham D 69 2
Newcastle Trolleybuses D 78 4
Newport (IOW) - Branch Lines to A 26 0
Newquay - Branch Lines to C 71 0
Newton Abbot to Plymouth C 60 4
Northern France Narrow Gauge C 75 8
North East German Narrow Gauge D 44 9
North Kent Tramways B 44 2
North London Line B 94 7
North Woolwich - BLs around C 65 9
Norwich Tramways C 40 6
Nottinghamshire & Derbyshire T/B D 63 0
Nottinghamshire & Derbyshire T/W D 53 1
O
Ongar - Branch Lines to E 05 5
Oxford to Bletchley D57 9
Oxford to Moreton-in-Marsh D 15 9
P
Paddington to Ealing C 37 6
Paddington to Princes Risborough C 81 9
Padstow - Branch Line to B 54 1
Peterborough to Kings Lynn
Plymouth - BLs around B 98 5
Plymouth to St. Austell C 63 5
Pontypool to Mountain Ash D 65 4
Porthmadog 1954-94 - BL around B 31 2
Portmadoc 1923-46 - BL around B 13 8
Portsmouths Tramways B 72 5
Portsmouth to Southampton A 31 4
Potters Bar to Cambridge D 70 8
Princes Risborough - Branch Lines to D 05 0
Princes Risborough to Banbury C 85 7
R
Reading to Basingstoke B 27 5
Reading to Didcot C 79 6
Reading to Guildford A 47 5
Reading Tramways B 87 9
Reading Trolleybuses C 05 5
Redhill to Ashford A 73 4
Return to Blaenau 1970-82 C 64 2
Rickmansworth to Aylesbury D 61 6
Romania & Bulgaria Narrow Gauge E 23 9
Roman Roads of Hampshire D 67 8
Roman Roads of Kent E 02 4
Roman Roads of Surrey C 61 1
Roman Roads of Sussex C 48 2
Romneyrail C 32 1
Ross-on-Wye - Branch Lines around E 30 7
Ryde to Ventnor A 19 2
S
Salisbury to Westbury B 39 8
Saxmundham to Yarmouth C 69 7
Saxony Narrow Gauge D 47 0
Scarborough Tramways E 15 4
Seaton & Eastbourne Tramways B 76 3
Seaton & Sidmouth - Branch Lines to A 95 6
Secret Sussex Resistance B 82 4
Selsey - Branch Line to A 04 8
Shepherds Bush to Uxbridge T/Ws C 28 4
Shrewsbury - Branch Line to A 86 4
Shrewsbury to Ludlow E 21 5
Shrewsbury to Newtown E 29 1
Sierra Leone Narrow Gauge D 28 9
Sirhowy Valley Line E 12 3
Sittingbourne to Ramsgate A 90 1
Slough to Newbury C 56 7
Solent - Creeks, Crafts & Cargoes D 52 4
Southamptons Tramways B 33 6
Southampton to Bournemouth A 42 0
Southend-on-Sea Tramways B 28 2
Southern France Narrow Gauge C 47 5
Southwark & Deptford Tramways B 38 1
South W Harbours - Ships & Trades E 22 2
Southwold - Branch Line to A 15 4
South London Line B 46 6
South London Tramways 1903-33 D 10 4
South London Tramways 1933-52 D 89 0
South Shields Trolleybuses E 11 6
St. Albans to Bedford D 08 1
St. Austell to Penzance C 67 3
Stourbridge to Wolverhampton E 16 1
St. Pancras to Barking D 68 5
St. Pancras to St. Albans C 78 9
Stamford Hill Tramways B 85 5
Steaming through the Isle of Wight A 56 7
Steaming through West Hants A 69 7
Stratford upon avon to Birmingham D 77 7
Stratford upon Avon to Cheltenham C 25 3
Surrey Home Guard C 57 4
Surrey Narrow Gauge C 87 1
Sussex Home Guard C 24 6
Sussex Narrow Gauge C 68 0
Swanley to Ashford B 45 9
Swindon to Bristol C 96 3
Swindon to Gloucester D46 3
Swindon to Newport D 30 2
Swiss Narrow Gauge C 94 9
T
Talyllyn - 50 years C 39 0
Taunton to Barnstaple B 60 2
Taunton to Exeter C 82 6
Tavistock to Plymouth B 88 6
Tees-side Trolleybuses D 58 6
Tenterden - Branch Line to A 21 5
Three Bridges to Brighton A 35 2
Tilbury Loop C 86 4
Tiverton - Branch Lines around C 62 8
Tivetshall to Beccles D 41 8
Tonbridge to Hastings A 44 4
Torrington - Branch Lines to B 37 4
Tunbridge Wells - Branch Lines to A 32 1
Twickenham & Kingston Trys C 35 2
U
Upwell - Branch Line to B 64 0
V
Victoria & Lambeth Tramways B 49 7
Victoria to Bromley South A 98 7
Vivarais Revisited E 08 6
W
Walthamstow & Leyton Tramways B 65 7
Waltham Cross & Edmonton Trys C 07 9
Wandsworth & Battersea Tramways B 63 3
Wantage - Branch Line to D 25 8
Wareham to Swanage - 50 yrs D 09 8
War on the Line A 10 9
Waterloo to Windsor A 54 3
Waterloo to Woking A 38 3
Watford to Leighton Buzzard D 45 6
Wenford Bridge to Fowey C 09 3
Westbury to Bath B 55 8
Westbury to Taunton C 76 5
West Cornwall Mineral Railways D 48 7
West Croydon to Epsom B 08 4
West German Narrow Gauge D 93 7
West London - Branch Lines of C 50 5
West London Line B 84 8
West Wiltshire - Branch Lines of D 12 8
Weymouth - Branch Lines around A 65 9
Willesden Junction to Richmond B 71 8
Wimbledon to Beckenham C 58 1
Wimbledon to Epsom B 62 6
Wimborne - Branch Lines around A 97 0
Wisbech - Branch Lines around C 01 7
Wisbech 1800-1901 C 93 2
Woking to Alton A 59 8
Woking to Portsmouth A 25 3
Woking to Southampton A 55 0
Wolverhampton Trolleybuses D 85 2
Woolwich & Dartford Trolleys B 66 4
Worcester to Birmingham D 97 5
Worcester to Hereford D 38 8
Worthing to Chichester A 06 2
Y
Yeovil - 50 yrs change C 38 3
Yeovil to Dorchester A 76 5
Yeovil to Exeter A 91 8
York Tramways & Trolleybuses D 82 1